Spiderwalk

Spiderwalk

The High Life and Daring Stunts of a Small-Town Girl from Arkansas

Ann "Annie" Miles

BUTLER CENTER BOOKS
LITTLE ROCK, ARKANSAS

BUTLER CENTER BOOKS

The Butler Center for Arkansas Studies
Central Arkansas Library System
100 Rock Street
Little Rock, Arkansas 72201
www.butlercenter.org

Hardcover ISBN: 978-1-945624-09-4
Paperback ISBN: 978-1-945624-10-0

Manager: Rod Lorenzen
Copyeditor: Ali Welky
Book and cover designer: H. K. Stewart

All photographs in this book are from the private collection of the author unless otherwise noted. The front cover photograph of the spiderwalk stunt is by Josh Weiner, New York (1973).

Printed in the United States of America.
This book is printed on archival-quality paper that meets requirements of the American National Standard for Information Sciences, Permanence of Paper, Printed Library Materials, ANSI Z39.48-1984.

Butler Center Books, the publishing division of the Butler Center for Arkansas Studies, was made possible by the generosity of Dora Johnson Ragsdale and John G. Ragsdale Jr.

To my friend
Lorena Carver,
owner and trainer
of the High Diving Horses

Contents

The Girl in Red 9

Acknowledgements 11

1. Atlantic City 13

2. Steel Pier 17

3. Leaving Home 25

4. Virginia Hotel 30

5. Fearless 34

6. Vance and Sonny 40

7. Leap of Faith 43

8. Diving Horses 101 49

9. Rock 'n' Roll Heaven 53

10. The Stars Come Out 57

11. Travelin' Man 61

12. Boardwalk Memories 66

13. Dangerous Waters 69

14. The Big Apple 72

15. Playboy Bunny 74

16. Show Biz 80

17. Stuntgirl 83

18. Imprints 89

19. Agent Interviews 91

20. Uncredited Stunt Work 99
21. Soap Operas 103
22. A New Leaf 106
23. *The Exorcist* 110
24. Surprise 115
25. Hairstyling and Barbering 118
26. Bob Kelly Wig Creations 122
27. Movie Hairstylist 124
28. Broadway 126
29. *Cats* and More 131
30. Spiderwalk 135
31. SAG-AFTRA 139
32. It's a Wrap 143
About the Author 145

The Girl in Red

Tribute to Lorena Carver

Lorena grew up traveling with the Wild West show her father W. F. "Doc" Carver performed with "Buffalo Bill" Cody. Her father was a world-renowned marksman in the 1800s. He and Cody shot buffalo on the plains together. That's where the name "Buffalo Bill" came from. Carver later said he regretted that, but he was young at the time and they were getting rich with it. After shooting for European royalty and becoming the world's greatest marksman, Carver formed a Wild West show with Cody. It didn't last long. They went separate ways, each with a show of his own.

Among other attractions, "Doc" had a diving horse in his show. Over the years, it was the diving horse that endured. His daughter Lorena was the first girl to ride the Carver High Diving Horses. When she was eleven years old, her father bet someone a hundred dollars she could ride a horse off a 60-foot tower. He won the bet, of course, and that's the way Lorena began her career in 1912. She became known as the "Girl in Red." She always wore a red bathing frock that looked almost like a dress. Modest, you know. Her father

Among other attractions, "Doc" had a diving horse in his show. Over the years, it was the diving horse that endured. His daughter Lorena was the first girl to ride the Carver High Diving Horses.

Lorena was way ahead of her time. She was a strong, independent woman and well loved on the pier.

insisted she be ladylike! However, she could ride a horse off a 60-foot tower. That was all right with him.

Lorena's brother Al had a difficult time getting along with his father. He ran away with the circus and became a roustabout. He was somewhat estranged from his father for a long time. He did return before his father's death. After their father's death, the tower was lowered to 40 feet and Lorena was not injured so often. Then they could hire other riders. Lorena had her unit of the act and Al had his unit. Lorena managed her act and still rode the horses. Around 1930, she quit riding but kept touring with girls she hired to ride. She came to the Steel Pier after George A. Hamid Sr. bought the pier in 1945.

Lorena was the owner-trainer of the High Diving Horses and would manage the act on the Steel Pier until she retired in the late '60s. A fire burned down the end of the pier—*again*.

Lorena was way ahead of her time. She was a strong, independent woman and well loved on the pier. She was a kind and generous person who was the backbone of the Carver High Diving Horse Act and the best rider ever.

Acknowledgements

I would like to thank the following people and organizations:

SAG-AFTRA—John McGuire and Leif Larson for helping me get verification.

Warner Bros. Pictures—Jane C. Lee for letter of acknowledgement.

***Arkansas Democrat-Gazette* (arkansasonline.com)**—David Bailey, Managing Editor; and Philip Martin, Features & Style editor, columnist, and chief movie critic, for "Miles from Famous" article, September 11, 2015.

***Pine Bluff Commercial* (pbcommercial.com)**—Amy Widner, Managing Editor; Michael Lee, Accent, for "PB Woman Reflects" article, June 14, 2015.

Butler Center for Arkansas Studies—Butler Center Books manager Rod Lorenzen for tracking me down and helping me all the way to publication. Ali Welky for much needed help and for being one of the best editors anywhere.

Princeton Antiques Bookshop—Robert E. Ruffolo Jr. for his vast knowledge of Atlantic City and his wonderful collection of photos. Also, for his humor and sharing and for my introduction to Atlantic City's Diving Horse lager beer.

Bloomsbury Publishing—Katie Gallof and Daniel Eagan for correction made in *America's Film Legacy 2009-2010.*

LeNelle Woods-Cobbs—my computer expert for her patience with me and her computer expertise.

All my friends, who supported me, gave me feedback, and put up with my jabber: Karen Polomsky, Jessie Morris, Celeste Morris, Shelly Kendall, Ashley Reed, BU and Bunchy and Allison Bertrand.

A special thanks to Deborah Noe and Celeste Morris, who nursed me through two major brain surgeries in 2016. Thanks to my doctors Shabbir Dharamsey and Ali Krisht. They are top notch. Three aneurysms found and clipped. Also, Dr. Roy Burrell for surgery on my writing hand. Thanks to these doctors, I am still here and still writing.

1.
Atlantic City

Atlantic City,
New Jersey,
was known
as America's
playground for
many, many years.

Atlantic City, New Jersey, was known as America's playground for many, many years. At the turn of the century, ladies and gents strolled the boardwalk in their best finery, with ladies wearing big hats with feathers.

This panoramic view of the boardwalk at Atlantic City, New Jersey, was taken before the palaces for legalized gambling were built in the 1970s. (Courtesy of Robert E. Ruffolo Jr.)

Two iconic businesses—Planters Peanuts and Fralinger's Salt Water Taffy—were located across the boardwalk from the Steel Pier. (Courtesy of Robert E. Ruffolo Jr.)

The Steel Pier opened in 1898. Before large palace-like hotels were built along the boardwalk, people came from New York, Philadelphia, all over New Jersey, and even Connecticut and stayed in boardinghouses that lined the streets leading off the boardwalk. There were no toilets in the rooms. There were toilets and showers in the hall, and on one floor there was a kitchen for all tenants to use. There were porches with rockers on all the boardinghouses. There were even porches and terraces on the Steel Pier. They had what they called sun parlors where people could just sit and read a book or gaze out to sea.

John Philip Sousa gave afternoon concerts on the Steel Pier, and later Broadway shows previewed there. In the '30s and '40s, there were big bands and dancing in the Marine Ballroom. Whatever was hot was hotter on the Steel Pier.

After the big hotels were built, wealthy tourists and politicians congregated in Atlantic City for business and for vacation. Maybe you saw Terence Winter's *Boardwalk Empire*. His Nucky character stayed at the Ritz-Carlton Hotel. That was on the boardwalk in the '20s when Prohibition was the law of the land—but not for Nucky. He was a bootlegger. Big time!

I guess about everyone knows the Miss America contest is held at the convention hall in Atlantic City. Many more things have been held there, too—like a Beatles concert in the '60s, the 1964 Democratic Convention, and the Ice Capades.

There were seafood restaurants and tourist sites in addition to the beach and the boardwalk. In the old days, they had little wicker rickshaws that were pushed instead of pulled on the boardwalk. You could be pushed along the boards in these rolling chairs—a way of seeing and being seen.

In the old days, they had little wicker rickshaws that were pushed instead of pulled on the boardwalk. You could be pushed along the boards in these rolling chairs—a way of seeing and being seen.

Fralinger's Original Salt Water Taffy had a taffy-pulling machine in their window so you could see the taffy being made. Planters Peanuts was next door, and Mr. Peanut stood outside the

Battery-operated rolling chairs cruised the boardwalk during the 1950s. (Courtesy of Robert E. Ruffolo Jr.)

door to greet tourists as they walked by. There was an atmosphere on the boardwalk in Atlantic City that put your soul at ease. There was no place like it, and the Steel Pier was just wonderful. For one low admission, you could go onto the pier, stay all day, and still not see everything. People came back year after year and had to see the World Famous High Diving Horses, the featured act on the Steel Pier. Everyone knew about it. Everyone wanted to see it. The Steel Pier really was the SHOWPLACE OF THE NATION! Songs were written like "On the Boardwalk in Atlantic City," and the game of Monopoly was fashioned after the Atlantic City boardwalk. The World Famous High Diving Horses act was Atlantic City's premier attraction for years and years.

People came back year after year and had to see the World Famous High Diving Horses, the featured act on the Steel Pier. Everyone knew about it. Everyone wanted to see it.

I wore my one Sunday outfit and high heels, which I would regret.

2.
Steel Pier

I wore my one Sunday outfit and high heels, which I would regret. I packed a suitcase with everything else I owned, which wasn't much: jeans, a bathing suit, shirts, underwear, and a sweat suit. When I arrived in Atlantic City, the airport seemed a little desolate and de-

The Steel Pier in Atlantic City, New Jersey, was a popular vacation spot for tourists.

serted. I got my bag and then got into a taxi cab. I said, "I'm going to the Steel Pier." The driver knew exactly where to go and, all the way in, I saw billboards with STEEL PIER—SHOWPLACE OF THE NATION and a drawing of the famous diving horse. The billboards were huge and all over the place. I got butterflies in my stomach just thinking about it. I was going to ride that horse! When the cab driver found out I was going to ride the diving horse, he seemed thrilled. He took me to Virginia Ave., parked the car, and carried my suitcase up the ramp to the Steel Pier entrance and wished me good luck. I checked in at the employees' entrance and was directed to walk to the end of the Steel Pier, where Lorena Carver would be expecting me.

Ann with Gamal, her favorite horse.

It was a half mile out to the end of the Steel Pier. Since it was the beginning of the season, there weren't many people on the pier yet. I started walking on the outside. It was like a boardwalk, and I had on three-inch heels and was carrying a suitcase. My heels kept getting stuck in the cracks so I moved inside. There were venders, games, and rides, and it was like being at a carnival with cotton candy and everything. I passed the two theaters where they showed movies and had stage shows with all the big-name stars of the day. Then, I came to the Marine Ballroom. It was huge with windows opened to the sea on both sides. There was a stage on one end where famous big bands of yesterday used to play into the night

When the cab driver found out I was going to ride the diving horse. he seemed thrilled. He took me to Virginia Ave.. parked the car. and carried my suitcase up the ramp to the Steel Pier entrance and wished me good luck.

for patrons to dance. There was a diving bell outside that took customers under the sea. I was getting the idea, as I looked around, that fate had picked me up and put me down in a wonderful, colorful historic place.

On past the ballroom was the water show with the famous diving horse as its featured act. I got to the entrance and there was a stairway up to the sound booth. Jerry the sound man stood outside on a little porch looking down at me.

At this point, it was all chained off, with DO NOT ENTER signs, and I could see the diving horse tower above the sound booth, in the background. Jerry said, "Hi, doll, I'm Jerry. Are you the new rider?" I told him I hoped I would be. I said, "My name is Annie and I'm looking for Miss Carver." He said to give him a minute and he'd take me to her. He went inside, shut the music off, locked the door, and came down. He took my suitcase and walked me beyond the chain into the backstage area to a room where Lorena was sitting behind her desk with a miniature gray poodle at her feet. Jerry did the introduction and left with, "This is your new rider."

Accident Inspired Diving Horse Act

INCLUDED IN YOUR ONE LOW ADMISSION

From the tower 40 feet above the heads of thousands of spectators at Steel Pier, the world-famous High Diving Horse will make his spine-tingling leap into a tank below, four or five times a day.

As you watch his amazing plummet, you will be seeing history in the making. This is the 50th anniversary of Steel Pier's most famous, most incredible act.

The High Diving Horse has been acclaimed by Life and other national magazines. Hardly a newspaper in the country has failed to featurize this breath-taking entertainment thriller. Outstanding stars of radio, television and movies talk about the High Diving Horse as a member of the most exclusive entertainment fraternity.

Watching the fearless steed and his lovely bareback rider has been the climax of a full day's entertainment for millions of Steel Pier visitors. Always, there is the gasp, "How did this amazing act start? Who had the wild imagination to jump a horse 40 feet? How does the horse survive the plunge?"

This miraculous entertainment feat actually began as the result of a near-fatal accident. Fifty years ago, Dr. W. F. Carver, a noted plainsman and champion rifle shot of the world, was returning home one stormy night. He was crossing a rickety bridge over a raging river. Suddenly, the bridge collapsed, plunging horse and rider 40 feet into the water. Fortunately both swam to safety. Back home and seated by the fireplace in fresh warm clothing, Dr. Carver kept thinking over and over, "Could this work again? Can a horse be trained to survive this same drop it had lived through in the accident?"

The circus-bred entertainer tried hundreds of horses and devised many training schemes. Finally, he perfected the dive and to his beautiful daughter, Lorena, he assigned the hazardous, but thrilling position of riding the High Diving Horse.

The rest is history. Grandparents tell youngsters about the High Diving Horse. Story-tellers on television repeat its fame.

When you go out to the end of the vast pier to catch the High Diving Horse in action, be sure and watch for the lady who gives him a carrot for a reward when he swims out of the tank. She is none other than Lorena Carver, the first rider of the High Diving Horse. She's following in her father's footsteps now as the remarkable trainer of High Diving Horses.

This article describes how the diving horse act evolved and shows Ann with Lorgah, whom she also called "Big Boy."

Lorena was warm and welcoming. She had on a summer dress that was a little off-the-shoulder, showing a butterfly tattoo (before everybody had tattoos). Her glasses looked like a butterfly, too, and had rhinestones. She wore a Victorian tiger claw necklace and her shoes were wedges. She was in her eighties, as I would learn later, and sharp as a tack. She smoked KOOLS, and I thought she was cool. I liked her immediately.

She told me things to be careful about, like the fact that the horse will throw his head back just before he hits the water. So, you have to duck to one side or he hits you in the face.

She offered coffee, which I gladly took. I hadn't eaten all day except for nuts and a Coke on the plane. We talked about my trick horseback riding, my college gymnastics, and my high diving and aerial work. Then, she said I could watch the next show and tomorrow I could ride a horse off the low tower. There was a chute about halfway up the tower that was used to train the horses. I was to start on that.

Then I met the stage manager, a stagehand, and some of the performers in the high diving act—mostly college students like me. I met Norma Dean, who was a champion high diver and, at present, rode the diving horse. It wasn't her favorite thing to do, and she was happy to be finished, I think. She told me things to be careful about, like the fact that the horse will throw his head back just before he hits the water. So, you have to duck to one side or he hits you in the face. When he kicks off the tower, it's a real jolt, so you have to make sure you have a good grip and hold on tight. If you don't duck your head at entrance, the water slaps you in the face and you'll end up with black eyes from that height.

A group of divers who performed comedic stunts pose before going to work.

I asked her if there was a place for me to change clothes. I wanted to get out of the high heels and straight skirt. She let me use her dressing room. I put on my sneakers and a sweat suit. Much better! I wouldn't have to walk the half mile back off the pier in high heels. By this time, I was starving and had a headache from not eating and being in the sun all afternoon.

Clowning with Russ Dodson, Ann's coach for high diving into the ocean.

Much has been written about the Steel Pier in the early days before World War II. The '20s and '30s were the years of big bands and dancing in the Marine Ballroom. W. F. "Doc" Carver is known as the originator of the diving horse act and father of both Lorena and Al Carver. After his death in 1927, Lorena and Al toured the country with their high diving horses. Al married his rider Sonora Webster in 1928. In 1929, Al and Sonora were booked on the Steel Pier. They were there for four years. They went back on the road in 1932, and Sonora rode for ten more years after she had been blinded in 1931. They retired for good in 1942.

These were the World War II years, and it was difficult to get workmen for the pier. The hotels were all filled with servicemen. Sometimes there were blackouts at night. It got so bad for a while it looked like the pier would close. Thankfully, it didn't, but there was a long period of time when there was no diving horse act on the pier. In 1944, a devastating hurricane blew away the end of the pier where the diving horses had been.

When I started riding in 1958, Norma Dean—a champion diver performing with the diving act—was riding the horse. All the other girls had retired by 1957, and Norma left shortly after I arrived.

It was 1945 when George A. Hamid Sr. purchased the Steel Pier. He rebuilt the end of the pier beyond the Marine Ballroom. He built a large stadium that looked across the ocean to the stage area where he put a horse tower and tank. Circus acts were booked for his water circus. He had arranged for Lorena Carver to bring back the diving horses. When Lorena came back, she had many riders before my time.

When I started riding in 1958, Norma Dean—a champion diver performing with the diving act—was riding the horse. All the other girls had retired by 1957, and Norma left shortly after I arrived. Marion Hackney covered for me when I was sent to do other appearances. For my first few years, I was still using my maiden name, Ann Eastham. I would then continue to ride through the '60s under my professional name, Ann Miles.

This group of "diving collegians," including Norma Dean (center), completes its routine.

Marion, who retired in 1957, still came to visit Lorena often, and I got to know her. She was likable, friendly, and popular. Her father Joe Hackney dove from a blimp in 1945 when Hamid bought the pier. He was still in the diving act a couple of years after I started riding.

By the late '60s, audiences were falling off again. Lorena retired at the end of the decade, and the diving horse act lost luster when she was gone and there was nobody there to train horses. A fire in 1969 burned down the beautiful Marine Ballroom and the whole end of the pier. The end of the pier was built back but was never the same. The focus became amusements and rides rather than live entertainers. Now the pier was plagued with storms and fires. A tent they called the Golden Dome replaced the Marine Ballroom, and the end of the pier was reconfigured.

Ann shares a dinner break with a group of high-wire walkers.

George Hamid Jr. sold the pier to investors in 1973. They took control in 1976. The investors dove a horse for three years but could not make a go of it. The last horse dove in 1978. Sadly, the pier had been neglected and was in bad shape. There was not a water circus to speak of. The audiences fell off until they were no longer there. The Steel Pier's glory days were over. One last fire destroyed all of the pier. A new Steel Pier was built on a much smaller scale and mostly featured amusement rides.

By this time, gambling casinos were taking over the boardwalk. The beautiful grand hotels were demolished and replaced with casinos. The boardinghouses were demolished and turned into parking lots. To me it was heartbreaking. Gambling lasted only a few years and left Atlantic City demolished and devastated. I was lucky to be there in the good times—the rock 'n' roll years.

The Steel Pier is gone now, as are Lorena Carver and the high diving horses. George Hamid Sr. and George Hamid Jr. and Lorena

People all over the country have fond memories of the Steel Pier.

Carver are people I have known. May they rest in peace. People all over the country have fond memories of the Steel Pier. I also have fond memories of the pier and the larger-than-life personalities who ran it for thirty-plus years.

3.
Leaving Home

I had not left home in Arkansas under the best circumstances. My parents said, "You're not going!" I said, "Oh yes, I am!" I don't think anyone could have stopped me.

I had not left home in Arkansas under the best circumstances. My parents said, "You're not going!" I said, "Oh yes, I am!" I don't think anyone could have stopped me. I was 17 years old, almost 18. I had been away from home for a year already. I was in college at Florida State University on a gymnastics scholarship. I was going to Atlantic City, New Jersey, for my 1958 summer job. It seemed normal to me. I had to support myself and pay for my education.

It didn't enter my mind that my riding a horse off a 40-foot tower probably scared my parents to death. They didn't say that. They listened to my aunts who said, "Nice southern girls don't go traipsing around the country all by themselves." Well, I was a nice southern girl and I did.

My brother, David, was a year and a half older than me. He played the guitar and was a cartoon artist. We both loved rock 'n' roll. If Elvis was anywhere in Arkansas doing a concert, David would get there somehow. This was before Elvis became a huge star. It didn't help that Orval Faubus, governor of Arkansas, was on TV all the time saying that rock 'n' roll was corrupting the young folks.

It was the late '50s, and our family was the typical family with conservative family-type values. We must have kept my parents on pins and needles all the time. The only saving grace was that my mom and dad both had a good sense of humor—once they got over the fear that we were morally bankrupt… Later, when we got some attention for our creative efforts, they could even brag a little on us if someone else brought up the subject.

Even when we were very little we were always up to something. When I was three or four years old, I jumped out of our neighbor's hayloft onto a haystack below. Every time I saw a haystack there from then on, I went over. That's how I learned to "cut a flip," as I would say. Nobody ever figured out what I was talking about.

When I was three or four years old, I jumped out of our neighbor's hayloft onto a haystack below. Every time I saw a haystack there from then on, I went over. That's how I learned to "cut a flip," as I would say. Nobody ever figured out what I was talking about.

In those days, Maw Maw (my mother's mother) lived with us, and she was in a wheelchair. My brother would make a cardboard sign that said *Maw Maw's Hotrod* and hang it on the back of her wheelchair. Then he put cardboard pieces on her spokes with clothespins. Once, when the preacher dropped by, she met him at the door in her "hotrod." She didn't know, of course. Anyway, David was the apple of her eye. As far as she was concerned, he could do no wrong. We all survived this stuff and lots more. We laughed about it years later.

When I was five years old, we moved into town (Malvern, Arkansas) and Daddy got a restaurant called the Aqua Dinette. It was in connection with a motel and swimming pool owned by Mr. Pete.

My mom was the best cook in town. Everyone said so. She made 40 pies a day for the restaurant. She would make a big dish pan full of crust at home each night and take it to the restaurant the next morning where she made all flavors of pies. People came from all over Arkansas to have pie and coffee at the Aqua Dinette in Malvern. Some would buy a pie to take home with them. When they came back, they brought the pan and took another pie.

David and I got to hang out in the kitchen. If we behaved ourselves, Mother took us swimming before we went home. Daddy had this restaurant for years and as we got older we went to the pool by ourselves.

David got an electric guitar and soon enough I discovered the high diving board. I still couldn't swim and I couldn't do an approach yet, but I would go to the end of the board, get a little spring going, then jump off the board, doing as many flips as I could before I hit the water. I got smacked around pretty good, but it didn't matter. I would dog-paddle to the rope and pull myself to the edge of the pool so I could get out and do it again. Some high school kid eventually taught me to swim, and I was learning to high dive. I was doing gymnastics before I even knew what it was. I saw it on TV. I used a rail fence for my balance beam. Tumbling and contortion work just came naturally to me. I called it acrobatic dancing. I did it in talent shows at school and later in benefit shows or on TV in Little Rock.

I was doing gymnastics before I even knew what it was. I saw it on TV. I used a rail fence for my balance beam. Tumbling and contortion work just came naturally to me. I called it acrobatic dancing.

In junior high school, our physical education department got a trampoline. It was locked most of the time because there was nobody to teach it. That was really frustrating to me! Once in a while they unlocked it and let us jump a little if there was someone there to watch us. That was my introduction to the trampoline.

Later, at Florida State University (FSU), I had expert, champion teachers and because of my high diving, I progressed rapidly on the trampoline. It was one of my favorite events. At that time (1957) FSU was the best gymnastics school in the country. There were Olympic gymnasts on our team. We all used the trampoline to learn tricks for tumbling and other gymnastic events. Our gym had the best equipment and two trampolines. We had safety belts and everything needed to learn advanced tricks. Sometimes other Olympic gymnasts came there to work out because the gym was so well equipped.

In order to keep our scholarship, we were required to perform in a show called Gymkana. We chose partners for our acts and rehearsed for a few months before going on the road to other colleges that had booked our show to come to their campus.

I was asked to partner with two guys in the gym who were not on the gym team but were trampoline champions. They came from a circus background, and the difficulty of their tricks would make your jaw drop. I didn't know this at the time. I had just arrived on campus and was flattered that anyone would want to work with me. I was inexperienced and eager to learn. These guys were experienced and did not tolerate fear or indulge excuses. I didn't have any, so we got along, but they were relentless and drove me hard.

I could already do some basic trampoline tricks from learning my high diving. I didn't see anything—I just did it from feel and instinct. The first thing they taught me was where to look so I could see how to adjust if I was over or under. Then they put me in a safety belt and started teaching me back double somersaults. When I could stick the somersault and stand up, they put me in a twisting belt and taught me back layout somersaults with a full twist.

I could already do some basic trampoline tricks from learning my high diving. I didn't see anything—I just did it from feel and instinct. The first thing they taught me was where to look so I could see how to adjust if I was over or under.

They didn't tell me this was all leading to the point where I was supposed to land these tricks on their shoulders. I got to the point where I did them out of the belt and could stand on my own. Then they explained: In order for me to get enough height to land on their shoulders, they would "goose the bed" by applying their weight to mine at just the right moment so I could go twice as high with no effort. I couldn't use the belt because it would be in the way. The first time they did it, it scared the hell out of me. I didn't attempt to do a trick. It was all I could do to keep my balance and land. They slacked off a little on the goose, and I started doing the tricks and trying to land on their shoulders. I would land on their shoulders but couldn't stand up, or I would land just my toes then slide down their back. They complained I was hitting their ears. They would say, "Look where your feet are going and open your legs!" The worst was when I landed with my shins on their shoulders. These workouts went on for hours. When I left the gym, my shins were bloody sometimes and had knots the size of hen's eggs.

Finally one day I said, "I can't do this anymore! I'm too beat up and I still have to work three more days a week on my gymnastics!" My abs were so sore I had to climb the stairs to class backwards. They told me to let them think about it. I said, "I'm done." The next week they brought a teeter board into the gym. Oh my word… Now what? I'd never been on a teeter board in my life. I said, "If you think I'm going to land on your shoulders off a teeter board you are crazy!" They said, "No, no, no! Nothing like that. You will do your tricks that you have already learned and we will catch you in a sitting position." Long story short, they did a couple of tricks, I did a couple of tricks, then for our finale they had a ladder maybe three or four feet tall with a platform on top. They both got on the platform and jumped off together and kicked me up 15 or 20 feet. I did a layout piked front somersault. They ran over and both caught me. It was the most popular act in our show. All I had to do was fly. I was good at that. They never gave me any compliments or told me I did a good job, but when they introduced me, they would say, "This is our partner, Annie. She flies like a bird." It made my day.

They both got on the platform and both jumped off together and kicked me up 15 or 20 feet. I did a layout piked front somersault. They ran over and both caught me. It was the most popular act in our show.

Later this training made my stunt work seem like child's play. High falls were easy. Commercials on the trampoline were just basic and simple for me. FSU also had a circus program. You could take it and get a credit for one semester. After that you participated if you wanted to. I took it for one semester and learned flying trapeze. I majored in dance, so my physical calendar was overflowing. After that circus semester I just stuck to gymnastics and trampoline.

4.
Virginia Hotel

Lorena took me off the pier to the Virginia Hotel, where we had dinner in the bar and I met Paul, owner of the hotel-motel. When Paul renovated the hotel and added a motel, he left one wing of the hotel untouched and rented it only to performers. I got a room in that wing. It looked like something out of a B-movie, with a sink in the room and a shower in the bathroom down the hall. But it was cheap and only a half block from the pier. It had windows that looked out onto Virginia Avenue. The carpet was old and worn thin in places, but the iron bed had clean white sheets and a new chenille bedspread. It would be just fine, and the food downstairs was delicious.

I was beginning to realize this wing of the Virginia Hotel was one of the few old rooming houses left from Atlantic City's past when tourists came there from cities like Philadelphia, New York, and Trenton. These were working stiffs who could not afford the grand hotels that lined the boardwalk. Paul was preserving history. The large hotels on the boardwalk were the first to have bathrooms in the rooms. They attracted gangsters and celebrities of the day, as well as wealthy tourists.

When Paul renovated the hotel and added a motel, he left one wing of the hotel untouched and rented it only to performers. I got a room in that wing. It looked like something out of a B-movie, with a sink in the room and a shower in the bathroom down the hall.

Lorena Carver, whose father invented the diving horse act, visits with Gamal and Ann.

A rigorous workout on the beach was part of Ann's routine.

After I checked in and got my room key, Lorena and I walked back to the pier for the last show of the evening. The groom brought the horse back stage from a stall behind the ballroom. I got to see everything up close. The rig on the horse was like my trick-riding rig—a strap with hand holds. He wore a halter and seemed gentle enough. I was relieved.

I would watch the show from the audience that night and ride a horse in the morning. There were animal acts, trapeze artists, wire walkers, and the Steel Pier Diving Collegians. All of these acts led up to the famous Steel Pier high diving horse act. Norma climbed the ladder up the side of the tower as the emcee, Jack Montez, announced Gamal, the famous diving horse. At the top, Norma mounted and after a slight pause, the horse slid his front legs down the apron and kicked off the tower. It was over in a flash, but what a thrill! The splash was so big that people in the front two rows of the audience got a bath. They didn't mind, and I found out later that some of the regulars would take those seats on purpose. Young people felt like they were in the act if they got wet. Lots of teens came to the pier. In those days, Dick Clark did *American Bandstand* from the ballroom so it was the center of rock 'n' roll in its beginnings. They did all the dances of the day, like the mashed potato, the twist, and I don't know how many more.

It was hard getting to sleep that night with so much going on in my head, but I decided I didn't want to go off the low tower. I'd go right to the top. I went down the hall and took a hot shower. Finally, clean and exhausted back in my room, I slept like a baby.

Ann puts Gamal through a workout along the beach.

I was amazingly calm. I didn't feel any fear at all until I started climbing the ladder. Then I had butterflies and a big adrenalin rush. It was the first time it dawned on me that I had not prepared for this at all. I hadn't even climbed the ladder before.

5.
Fearless

Next morning, I woke with the sun streaming in my windows. I went down to the bar, which wasn't open for business yet, but Paul told me about the drugstore on the boardwalk right in front of the pier that had a lunch counter. I had an awesome breakfast. Some of the high divers were there eating and I got acquainted. I was going to like this place! Mr. Peanut stood on the boardwalk in front of Planters Peanuts. Right next door was Fralinger's Salt Water Taffy store, with a candy-pulling machine in the window. The first show wasn't until around eleven a.m., so I had an hour or so to tell Lorena I had decided I should go to the top on my first dive. To my surprise, she said, "If you're going to do that, you may as well do it in the show." I suited up, and my first dive was in a sold-out show that very morning. The emcee was informed of the plan, along with stagehands, the horse groom, and everyone else, I guess.

I was amazingly calm. I didn't feel any fear at all until I started climbing the ladder. Then I had butterflies and a big adrenalin rush. It was the first time it dawned on me that I had not prepared for this at all. I hadn't even climbed the ladder before. Believe me, 40 feet looks a lot higher from the top looking down than from the bottom looking up. My legs turned to Jell-O. I got to the top and perched on the side of the chute. I hadn't counted on how loud the horse's hoofs would sound as he came running up the wooden platforms or how much the tower would shake under his weight.

He was there right next to me. I could feel the warmth of his body. The spray from his whinny sent a shock through my system, but the old familiar pungent horsey smell put me at ease. It comforted me, and I realized I had been preparing for this moment all my life. With my heart in my throat, I jumped on and got a good grip. He didn't wait long but stood long enough to nod yes to the audience, then slid his hooves down the apron. I felt my ankles pressed between the horse and the tower as he kicked hard and I held on for dear life. A moment later, we hit the water. I ducked to the side with my head tucked on the side of his neck. WHAT A JOLT!

The spray from his whinny sent a shock through my system, but the old familiar pungent horsey smell put me at ease. It comforted me, and I realized I had been preparing for this moment all my life.

Underwater I let go with my legs. He hit bottom and kicked up. Once he surfaced, I put my legs back down and rode him up the ramp and out of the water. Lorena met us at the top of the ramp, where I jumped off and took a bow, to wild screams and applause. Gamal got carrots. Jerry the sound man hung a star on my dressing room door. The worst was over—or so I thought. I didn't realize there were six horses and I'd just ridden the best of all. Gamal would remain my favorite for as long as I rode—the next nine years.

The second time up I rode Phantom. He stood on the tower a long time. My adrenalin had calmed down a bit, and I had time to look down and see how high it really was. I thought, "*Holy shit… What have I gotten myself into?*" I couldn't linger long because he backed up, did a little prancy dance, then lunged forward and slid his hoofs halfway down the apron. Finally he was going. But no, wait. He got back up somehow and stood longer. I don't mind telling you, this was making me nervous. Eventually he did the dive, and it was fine.

I rode four shows a day, seven days a week. The first two weeks every season, I was so sore all over that I could hardly move—and I was in shape then! It didn't take long to get used to it, though.

I went through six horses the first two weeks I was there, and each one was unique. Each had his own routine. Black Beauty always hit a belly buster. Dimah went in so steep and kicked off so hard it gave me a headache every time. He was an accident waiting to happen. He never waited for me to mount. Instead, I had to jump for him as he passed. He was so keyed up and spooky that I finally refused to ride him my second year there. Lorgah was so big that I had a hard time getting my legs around his belly. Gamal was so sweet and gentle and always did a wonderful dive. Phantom was up and down, on and off. Patches was a smaller version of Lorgah.

I rode four shows a day, seven days a week. The first two weeks every season, I was so sore all over that I could hardly move—and I was in shape then! It didn't take long to get used to it, though. Once I was used to it, I'd be riding on the beach to exercise the horses before show time and jumping off the end of the pier to go water-skiing from pleasure boats that came around. Sometimes I'd swim to the beach and back between shows. Or some of the diving champions would coach me in high diving into the ocean. Russ Dodson was my coach for that, and he liked teaching me because he said I would do whatever he told me to. Sometimes, there were schools of jellyfish in the ocean and they got into my bathing suit. Other times, there were large waves and I had to time my diving according to the waves. Not so easy!

The horses dove into a tank that was set up on the deck. It was about fifteen or twenty feet in diameter and nine feet deep. The tower I started on in 1958 was a wooden tower with ramps for the horse to gallop up. Later, around 1962, after a huge storm washed the tower and tank out to sea, they replaced the wooden tower with a metal one that was put together in pieces and secured to the deck with guy wires. It had an elevator for the horse. I climbed a 40-foot ladder four times a day. This tower shook even worse than the old tower!

Funny thing was, I really wasn't scared on the tower—oh, enough to be careful, sure, but not more than that. I think all my experience to that point made me feel confident. To my way of thinking, the fun and excitement of it far outweighed any danger. After a while, I got so comfortable up there, I had to remind myself to be careful. After all, they were horses and could be distracted by, say, Clyde Beatty's lions and tigers left on stage below (in a cage of course). The horses freaked out when they got their scent, and I had some moments with my heart in my throat until that was taken care of. There were storms and hurricanes, too. Lorgah was the heaviest horse, so he was the one I rode when a storm was approaching and there were strong winds that shook the tower. How foolhardy is that?

Ann and her horse prepare to take off from the top of the 40-foot tower.

Once, in a night show, Gamal—the horse I never had trouble with—refused to dive until a workman noticed that a light was out by the tank and replaced it. The last show of the evening was always eerie. It was dark except on the tower and the tank. One time after a hurricane, I made a dive where the tower shook so badly I thought it was going over. When the tower was inspected, it was found that one of the main supports was sheared in two. These are things I had very little, if any, control over but learned to at least

Ann and Dimah in mid-air.

Truth is, I loved what I did. It wasn't all sweetness and light, though. We (the divers and I) got fungus in our ears from being in the water so much, and nights were cold. We all could relate to freezing our butts off every night.

try to be aware of. Truth is, I loved what I did. It wasn't all sweetness and light, though. We (the divers and I) got fungus in our ears from being in the water so much, and nights were cold. We all could relate to freezing our butts off every night. A reporter once asked, "Isn't it dangerous riding the horse at night or diving in the ocean?" I told him it was all dangerous, but when you do it all day and into the night 24/7, you get really good at it.

I didn't have it as bad as the divers. At least I just had to dive once with the horse, and the water in the tank wasn't quite as cold as the ocean. The divers did three or more dives at the beginning of the show, then they did a comedy act at the end. By the time they finished, they were frozen. Sometimes they would stand close to the lights on stage just to keep warm.

Most of my waking hours during this time were spent doing gymnastics, trampoline, trapeze, swimming, diving, and riding horses. It is definitely thrilling to have 1,500 pounds of hard-muscle horse flesh underneath you, perched 40 feet up on a tower as he slips his hoofs over the edge. You feel his muscles tense, and your muscles tense in response. You become one with your partner for a brief time, as you would in an acrobatic hand-balancing act. All your senses are magnified. You can relax and let the skills you have already learned take over. It's an instinctual dance. As he shifts his weight, you adjust your position. You brace for the jolt that comes when he kicks hard off the tower and for a brief moment you feel the freedom of soaring through the air with this marvelous creature. Now you must move to the side and brace yourself for entry into the water. As he throws his head back, you duck forward and merge into the side of his neck. The water opens and closes on you with a powerful force. Under only nine feet of water—silence. He hits with just enough force to kick back to the surface. The water breaks his fall, and the bottom is covered with bags of sawdust. You can relax and let him find his way. If everything goes well, you ride up the ramp and take a bow. Reward received.

I was the only rider on the pier from 1958 to 1966. I normally did four shows a day, seven days a week. In 1967 and 1968, I was called back to ride when girls were injured or out for some reason. All in all, I was there about ten years.

It's an instinctual dance. As he shifts his weight, you adjust your position. You brace for the jolt that comes when he kicks hard off the tower and for a brief moment you feel the freedom of soaring through the air with this marvelous creature.

I chased that horse all over the pasture. He kicked, he bit, he did everything. But I finally got the halter on him. Then I had to figure out how to get up on him. He was not having it.

6. Vance and Sonny

When I was 14 years old, I was performing my acrobatics in talent shows. Vance, a local man who owned horses, was on one of these shows. He asked if I'd like to do trick riding. That was all I needed to hear. Vance had a trained Brahma bull and a horse named Ace. He performed in rodeos all over the country. He had an old horse that had been retired in the pasture for a few years. His name was Sonny and he was 14 years old—the same age I was. Vance told me if I could go out to the pasture and ride him back to the barn, he would be my horse. But I would have to train him and learn to trick ride.

I chased that horse all over the pasture. He kicked, he bit, he did everything. But I finally got the halter on him. Then I had to figure out how to get up on him. He was not having it. I somehow got him up under a little tree and after much scuffling around, managed to shinny up high enough to grab a branch and swing on. Now that I wanted him to move he just stood there. I reached up and broke off a little switch, and then we were off and running—but not to the barn. I only had a halter on him, but he was trained to neck rein. I finally got him to the barn.

Sometime later, battered and bruised, I had me a horse. Vance laughed and laughed. Vance was a tall, good-looking man with almost white hair and pale blue eyes. Lanky is the word that comes to mind when I think of him now. He always dressed in western gear and wore his hat most of the time. He got me a ring curb like the circus has and started showing me how to train my horse.

Sonny would jump over the ring at first, so we rigged an electric fence to keep him in. But I had to be careful not to get on it myself. Pretty soon, Vance brought me a whip and I learned to crack it and how to make Sonny take a bow after I jumped off. I spent quite a bit of time training the horse before I actually started to ride. Vance showed me lots of things about training horses. He got a big kick out of seeing me goof up. But when I'd master something and show it to him, he got a big kick out of that, too. He showed me how to open the barn and where everything was, and where the bull would be—and told me not to go near him when Vance wasn't there. Once, when he was training the bull, he put me on the bull's bare back. I was riding a Brahma bull! It showed me how much Vance trusted me (and himself).

Vance showed me lots of things about training horses. He got a big kick out of seeing me goof up. But when I'd master something and show it to him. he got a big kick out of that, too.

I could come and go as I pleased. Most times I wasn't there long before he'd be out leaning on the fence watching. By this time I could grab a handful of mane and swing up onto Sonny's back. In the beginning, Sonny would bite me anytime he got a chance. I had some fierce bite wounds, but it didn't discourage me. After a while, Sonny seemed to like me and if I fell off, he'd stop dead still in his tracks. I didn't even have to go to the pasture anymore. I'd just whistle and he'd come running. I always took carrots and sugar for him.

I was also getting up at four in the morning so I could sneak into the local swimming pool and practice my high diving. Then I'd walk up the hill to Vance's place and go down to the pasture to ride Sonny for a while before I had to get to school. Sometimes I'd just dangle my feet in the creek and talk to Sonny. Then, I'd come back after school to ride. I had perfected my act enough to ride in some local benefit shows. Vance had a rig made for me of a beautiful green suede and leather, a strap with foot holds and hand holds. There was a feather plume for Sonny's head. He looked gorgeous.

Vance thought I was ready to do real rodeos. So, he wrote a letter to some big rodeo people in Dallas. I was doing shows with him all over Arkansas now. We always did the local rodeo. I had learned to spin ropes, too. I learned from a man called Peg. He just had one leg—the other was a peg. But he sure could spin those ropes. He showed me how to work my bullwhip, too.

I've always regretted that I never could properly express my gratitude to Vance for what he did for me. I have often thought of him as someone who had a special, profound influence on my life. I wanted to let him know how much I appreciated him, but I was shy and timid and maybe a little in awe of him. At the time, I had no way of knowing that the things Vance taught me about horses and the chance he gave me to do trick riding would stand me in good stead for the rest of my life.

At the time. I had no way of knowing that the things Vance taught me about horses and the chance he gave me to do trick riding would stand me in good stead for the rest of my life.

7.

Leap of Faith

When I started riding the diving horses, people would always ask, "What does it feel like to ride that horse?"

In high school, my classmates called me crazy. When I started riding the diving horses, people would always ask, "What does it feel like to ride that horse?" They wondered: Was I scared or was I crazy or did I have a death wish?

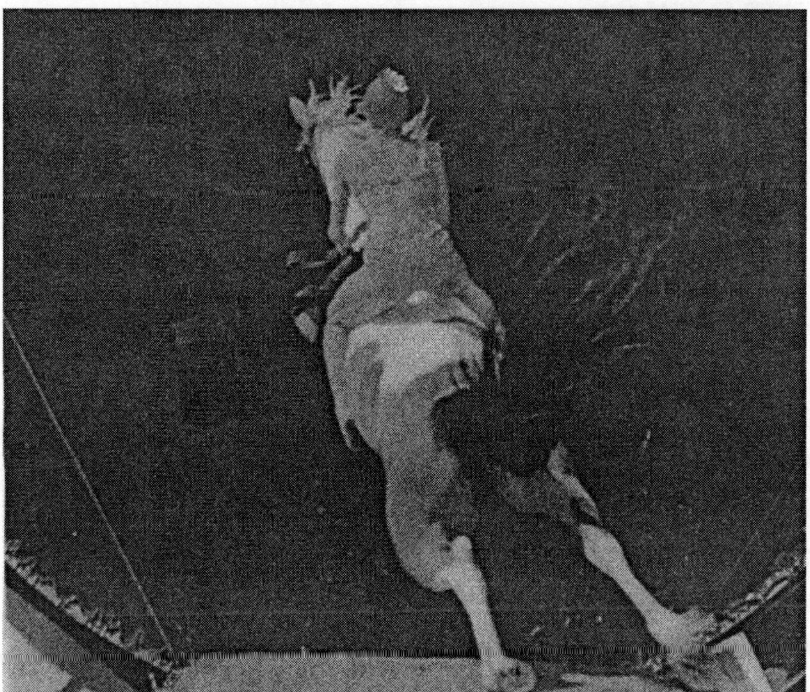

Shot from above the tower, Ann and her horse begin their descent from 40 feet high into a tank filled with nine feet of water. (Courtesy of Gabriel Gyorffy)

Am I crazy? Well, I've been called crazy all my life. I think I came close to believing it once or twice. I was a crazy kid, but I know what my classmates meant when they said I was crazy. They meant it would have been crazy for *them* to do the things I was doing. For them, it would have been but not for me. It was the most natural thing in the world for me to do. What does it feel like to do "crazy" stunts? It's another level of being in which the intensity of your senses is clear as a bell. It's inside the magic cocoon that Stanislavski speaks of in acting. It's being clothed in a protective blanket of warmth and light. It's the most exhilarating experience I've ever known. It's a rebirth, a place of such intense concentration that it washes you clean of everyday nuisance worries and puts things in perspective. It makes living in the moment really come true without a doubt. It is ecstasy! It's fun and happy and funny, and a bigger-than-life feeling. It puts a steel rod of sureness right down your spine that pins you to the center of the universe so that if you are on the ground, or 50 feet up, or 150 feet up, your ground or your floor is right underneath you. You know exactly where it is every minute. It's like living in another world, one that not everyone is so privileged to live in. Other acrobats know what I'm talking about. It's a Leap of Faith. How do you know you won't get hurt? You just do! That is, unless you change your mind mid-stream. You can't do that. FAITH…but, of course, you have practiced each step along the way. Your mind doesn't know what you're doing. You just do it physically, who knows why? Muscle memory? A gift from GOD? Divine guidance?

It's a rebirth, a place of such intense concentration that it washes you clean of everyday nuisance worries and puts things in perspective. It makes living in the moment really come true without a doubt. It is ecstasy!

You keep on doing it because it's natural for you to do it. Is that crazy? If you were playing the piano, and you were a child prodigy, would you be crazy then? I don't think so. Well, I didn't think so either when I wanted to jump off things and do flips and ride fast horses—or later, as a stunt person, get set on fire, jump out of three-story windows, ride in fast cars, go over a waterfall, or crash a car into the water. That's what I knew how to do and loved doing it. You can only do something well if you love it. I loved it, and it loved me.

Do I have a death wish? No, I have a life wish. I want to feel alive. I'd rather be anything than bored to death.

Do I have a death wish? No, I have a life wish. I want to feel alive. I'd rather be anything than bored to death.

Water, that's another thing I have always loved. I found another world in the water, too. If you're on top of it, it's full of sounds. It smacks you in the face, on your sunburn, and in your eyes, and challenges you to a good fight, but when you are underneath, it goes silent.

It is silent, but it is still alive. It has currents and caverns, plant growth, and all kinds of creatures and things you don't get to see in everyday aboveground life. You get to see things in another world—their world. It's like a constant hug from the water on every inch of your skin every second. It's not just another physical dimension, although it is that, too, but it's a higher mental/spiritual/emotional plane. I used to wonder why people thought athletes were dumb or shallow. I guess they didn't know that everything gets done with the brain. Did they think athletes were a body with no brain? If your brain doesn't send a signal first, your body can't follow. The only

Gamal, Ann's "sweetest" ride, soars off the tower.

Gamal and Ann make a smooth entry.

One time, Doc Carver was riding his horse over a bridge when the bridge collapsed. His horse jumped off the bridge and swam to shore. That's how the Carver High Diving Horses were born.

real reason for having a strong body is so you don't get hurt and so you are powerful and flexible enough to execute the brain's wish. I never saw a fish that was ashamed of itself, or a horse that ever lied to me... But people can make dogs ashamed, I think—just like people can make people ashamed.

People used to ask, "How do you make the horse do that?" My answer is, I don't. You don't make them do anything. You take 20 horses and see which ones are inclined to jump off a low platform. Then you weed out the ones who won't. You gradually increase the height, encouraging them to jump but never forcing them. They are trained from six months to a year before they take a rider. Some will not take a rider. They are all different, but most will do what a horse would do naturally, if put in that position.

This was discovered by W. F. "Doc" Carver, Lorena's father. He was the world champion rifle shot in the 1800s. He had the first Wild West show and partnered with Buffalo Bill before Buffalo Bill had his own Wild West show. One time, Doc Carver was riding his horse over a bridge when the bridge collapsed. His horse jumped off the bridge and swam to shore. That's how the Carver High Diving Horses were born.

Lorena started riding them on a bet when she was eleven years old in 1912. The tower was 60 feet high when Lorena rode. They lowered the tower to 40 feet before anyone else rode. Lorena was really the main rider in the early days. She was a celebrity in the '20s, when daredevils were all the rage. She knew movie stars and royalty. There were lots of other riders through the years, but none like Lorena.

About the same time Lorena was traveling with her father's show (around 1909) there was a little ragamuffin street acrobat in Lebanon. He was sent by his grandmother, who raised him after his mother's death to join his uncle's troupe of acrobats that traveled with Buffalo Bill's show. The show was in France at the time. Pahbla (nickname for George) would, as his grandmother knew,

Lorgah and Ann bob to the surface after another happy landing.

work his way to America, where he could escape the crushing poverty in Lebanon. George had maybe three years of schooling and spoke no English. He was nine years old but already a proficient tumbler. Since he was small, he would become the top man in his uncle's troupe of acrobats.

His uncle was somewhat harsh and did not look after George very well. Since he could not speak or understand English, George got pushed to the back of the line at mealtime and in general. He never got enough to eat. As luck would have it, Annie Oakley noticed him in the act and befriended him. She made sure he got enough to eat and taught him to read, write, and speak English. He has said Annie Oakley's smile was the first friendly face he saw in his new surroundings. Annie brought this situation to Cody's attention. It was arranged for George to get food until he understood how to manage for himself. Later, Cody drafted George to ride a horse in the opening of the show. He had never ridden a horse, but he learned.

After his stint with Buffalo Bill's show, George traveled the country with his own troupe of acrobats. They were making a meager living on the bookings he would manage to get for them. They ended up in Atlantic City, where they performed on the beach and slept at night under the Steel Pier. They would "pass the hat," as they say, and one fellow in the group had a girlfriend who brought them food from the restaurant where she worked as a waitress.

Eventually, George became a top booking agent for circus acts and started booking for the Million Dollar Pier and the Steel Pier. He owned a circus of his own that he also booked acts for. By the time I met him, he had owned and sold the Million Dollar Pier, renamed Hamid's Pier. He now owned the Steel Pier, the New Jersey State Fair, several theaters on the boardwalk, and who knows what else. This was George A. Hamid Sr. Now he was a wealthy man with a grown son, George Hamid Jr., who was primarily running the pier at this point. George Sr. still traveled the world to find the most sensational acts in the world for his water circus on the Steel Pier. At heart he was still that little acrobat who loved the circus.

Eventually. George became a top booking agent for circus acts and started booking for the Million Dollar Pier and the Steel Pier. He owned a circus of his own that he also booked acts for.

George Hamid Jr. was educated at Princeton and booked the rest of the performers for the pier. He was up to date and modern in his booking. They were both friendly and outgoing until it came to bargaining and money. Then they were as shrewd as shrewd can be.

8.
Diving Horses 101

GAMAL—an Arabian name meaning beautiful. He was my favorite horse in every way! Gamal was sweet and gentle. He would nuzzle me. He was the showman in the group. He always paused on the tower to nod yes before he dove. He was consistent and deliberate in his movements. He kicked just hard enough and went in at just the right angle. Easy ride! Underwater, he sometimes rolled but not often.

DIMAH—Hamid spelled backwards. I did not like Dimah! He was spooky and too spirited, always in a hurry. He never waited for me to mount. I had to jump for him as he passed. He kicked too hard off the tower and went in too steep. I always feared he would go over. Because he was named after Hamid, when one Dimah retired there was always another horse named Dimah.

LORGAH—The first three letters of Lorena's name, and the last three letters were George A. Hamid's initials. Lorgah was a big, heavy horse. I called him "Big Boy." He was a pleasure to ride. He seemed almost slow motion and went into the water smooth. You never felt a backbone riding Lorgah. What a big splash he made!

Lorgah was a big, heavy horse. I called him "Big Boy." He was a pleasure to ride. He seemed almost slow motion and went into the water smooth. You never felt a backbone riding Lorgah.

PHANTOM—What a piece of work! He had his own agenda and was stubborn. He would slide his front legs down the apron and just hang there. Then somehow he got back up on the tower and stood longer. Sometimes he did this more than once before he dove. It made me a nervous wreck the first time I rode him. After a few times, I knew he would do the same thing every time. One time there was a firemen's convention in town and a group of firemen were in the audience. After a while they started shouting, "It's okay, Phantom! You're not going to a fire."

BLACK BEAUTY—Just as his name implied, he was a beauty, but Beauty did not kick off hard enough, so halfway down his back legs would drop down and he would hit a sort of belly buster. He wasn't a very good swimmer either, but he seemed to enjoy it just the same. I had a hard time keeping my leg grip when his hind legs dropped, and he always rolled completely over underwater.

PATCHES—Patches was a smaller, sleeker version of Lorgah. He did a wonderful dive, and he was a real looker! He made postcards and book covers. He was always consistent and easy to ride.

I got to know all my horses, and they all had their own routine and stuck to it. They would throw their head back just before hitting the water, not underwater. It was murky under the water. I couldn't see much, but I didn't have to. Being under the water prevented fast movement, and I could always feel where I was. If it was necessary, I could put my feet on the horse and push away from him. I would release my legs and roll with them if they rolled. Unless the hoofs hit me in the head or face, it was no big deal. I wore a helmet when I first started riding, but I could never get used to it. It kept hitting my shoulder blade at impact with the water. I quit wearing it. I liked it better that way. Sometimes a horse would lean over with his weight on one side of the tower as he took off. I just lifted my

It was murky under the water. I couldn't see much. but I didn't have to. Being under the water prevented fast movement. and I could always feel where I was.

legs up and put them back down when he cleared the tower so I didn't get abrasions or worse.

As long as Lorena was there, these horses were well taken care of and never mistreated. Think about it. Why on earth would you want to be on a tower with a horse that was agitated? I know I wouldn't! Horses don't reason things out. They go on instinct. You can sometimes lead them on a rope until they get the idea, but you should never poke them with a prod or hit or kick or abuse them in any way. They do respond to kindness. Although animal rights were not as much of an issue in those days, the horses I rode were never abused.

Ann with Patches, one of the horses she rode for her act.

I was the only rider on the Steel Pier from 1958 through 1966. Although I normally did four shows a day seven days a week, the first day Ricky Nelson was on the pier in 1958, I did seven. There were a couple of years when I was out briefly doing appearances somewhere else. I think it was Marion Hackney who covered for me. After I retired in 1966, I went back a couple of times to cover when girls were injured. Basically Marion rode in the 1950s. I rode in the 1960s. I did not ride in the 1970s, as has been written. Names and dates are almost impossible to research. Some years there was more than one girl riding on the pier. They shared the shows. Girls came and went; horses came and went. Counting on news clips is not reliable because there is so much incorrect information in them. One of my news clips said the tower was 75 feet high and gave me Jayne Mansfield measurements. (I have no clue what that would have to do with diving a horse.) This same clip had several photos of me, then said I was only a substitute and another girl was the star of the show. I was never interviewed by this reporter. I have no idea where he got his false information. I was never a substitute! I certainly was not built like Jayne Mansfield. This kind of thing happened occasionally—just show biz sensationalism.

One of my news clips said the tower was 75 feet high and gave me Jayne Mansfield measurements. (I have no clue what that would have to do with diving a horse.)

9.

Rock 'n' Roll Heaven

After I got settled in and knew all my horses, I started to explore the Steel Pier. I could go anywhere I wanted, and it was all free. There was a small admission charge to get onto the pier, then you could stay all day if you wanted and still never see everything. There were two movie theaters that showed first-run movies of the day and they had a stage show afterward with all top stars: Phyllis Diller, Al Martino, Connie Francis, Brenda Lee, Joey Bishop, the Lennon Sisters, Dukes of Dixieland, the Four Aces, the Rolling Stones, Chuck Berry, Johnny Cash. Oh, my gosh—I can't remember all of them. Anyone who was anyone was there. I saw them all in person. Every two weeks or so they changed and another star came in. They came back between their stage shows to see our water show.

The Four Aces

George Hamid Jr. was primarily in charge of the pier, and I did all my business with him. He was the one who booked all the mu-

George was up to date or ahead of his time in knowing who to book. He has said his only regret was that he didn't book Elvis when he had the chance. He thought nobody would come to see someone named Elvis.

sicians, comics, etc. George was up to date or ahead of his time in knowing who to book. He has said his only regret was that he didn't book Elvis when he had the chance. He thought nobody would come to see someone named Elvis. He booked all the '50s teen idols—the artists I grew up hearing on the radio and my record player (45s and 78s): the Platters, Ricky Nelson, the Four Aces, Bill Haley, Patti Page, Connie Francis, and more. OH, WOW! I thought I'd died and gone to rock 'n' roll heaven. I got to meet most of the stars.

Our water circus (except for me) was booked by George Hamid Sr. Most of the other acts aside from the diving collegians and me stayed for a week or two, then another act came in. The divers and I were there for the whole summer every year. Some of the acts in our show were people like Clyde Beatty, the Walendas, and the Flying Alexanders. There were animal acts, a clown, dogs, seals, and an elephant. It was wonderful.

The diving champions did a straight diving act to open our show and a comedy diving act at the end—just before I rode the diving horse, there was a loud shotgun blast that went off at the end of the comedy diving. Everyone within hearing distance knew the diving horse was next and came out from the Marine Ballroom or wherever to see the horse dive. People came back over and over every summer.

I would go in the ballroom sometimes and dance "the Twist" when Chubby Checker was there. After a while, all the teen idols came back to see me. I was a teen and most of them were, too. I couldn't believe it! "Hello Darlin'…"—Conway Twitty was there, too. One of my favorites! We were pals. We had both lived in Arkansas. It was like we were old friends the first time we met. Now, the music of my life was up close and in person. I was in rock 'n' roll heaven! There was no place like the Steel Pier.

Some of the favorite songs of my growing up years were:

"Rock Around the Clock"—Bill Haley
"Sincerely"—McGuire Sisters
"Earth Angel"—The Platters
"Old Cape Cod"—Patti Page
"I'm Sorry"—Brenda Lee

Frankie Avalon

Bobby Rydell

Gene Krupa

My life was full of everything I loved: riding horses and dancing to the music of teen idols.

"Mr. Sandman"—The Four Aces

"Moments to Remember"—The Four Lads

"It's Only Make Believe"—Conway Twitty

My life was full of everything I loved: riding horses and dancing to the music of teen idols. The '50s and '60s for me were just a blast! I was in college at Florida State University on a gymnastics scholarship and my summer job was riding the diving horses on the Steel Pier in Atlantic City, New Jersey. What more could I ask for?

There was more to come!

Fabian

The Four Lads

The Lennon Sisters

10.
The Stars Come Out

For a while Dick Clark did American Bandstand in the ballroom. Between shows I would go watch sometimes. He came back stage to visit us at the water show, too.

I started riding when rock 'n' roll was the thing. For a while Dick Clark did *American Bandstand* in the ballroom. Between shows I would go watch sometimes. He came back stage to visit us at the water show, too. All the stars came out between shows. Our dressing rooms lined the end of the pier and we had them fixed for sunbathing on the flat roofs. We had barbecue grills, coffee makers, etc. I had a small refrigerator and an electric coffee pot in my room, and the workmen on the tower crew brought doughnuts and had coffee with me when they came to check the horse tower.

The big-name stars had dressing rooms like hotel suites, but they all seemed to prefer hanging out in our plywood rooms. Go figure.

One day after a show I was walking back to my dressing room, soaking wet from the dive, and waiting at my door was Louis Armstrong. He gave me a high five and said, "You a good rider. Where did you learn to ride like that?" I said that I guessed it was the same place he got his chops, and I pointed to heaven. We had a great laugh! He had a hanky with knots tied at the corners and placed on top of his head. When I asked about it he said it was to keep the sun off his head. I told him he was welcome to sit in my

Ann helped host a watermelon party that included Dick Clark, star of the popular dance program American Bandstand. *Clark is pictured with the author (middle of back row).*

room anytime he wanted so he could leave the door open and see outside. He told me I didn't have to call him Mr. Armstrong. He said I could call him Louis or Satchmo. I called him Louis. He called me Annie. We had a long talk, and he hung out in my room quite a bit. His joy for life and natural humor were just infectious. No wonder everyone loved him, not to mention his awesome talent! I was honored to be his friend (acquaintance, really). My favorite was when he sang "What a Wonderful World." I met lots of celebrities. Most of them briefly just to pass a few words, but some, like fellow Arkansan Conway Twitty, I actually got to know.

When the Three Stooges were appearing in the theater, they would come back between shows and hang out with us. For those of you too young to remember the Stooges—they were the most popular and most famous slapstick comedy team since the Marx

Brothers. They did many movies and all kinds of special appearances. They worked from the '20s through the late '60s.

One day they told me they were going to do a little show for the children in one of the local hospitals. They wanted to know if I would come along. They thought the kids would like to meet the diving horse rider. I said "sure." Then they asked if I could do some kind of little act. I said I could do an acrobatic dance.

On our dinner break I put on a leotard under my clothes and went with them to the hospital. I thought I'd do a few cartwheels, some walkovers, splits, etc., and meet the kids and then the Stooges would do a real show. They called me their opening act, but as soon as I started they were right out there with me. They had a brawl going on behind me everywhere I went around the floor. They fought about which horse I rode, hit each other on the head, poked each other's eyes, ran around me, and one-upped each other about who knew me best and said that I let one of them pet the horse and not the others. The kids were laughing and screaming, and I could

They called me their opening act, but as soon as I started they were right out there with me. They had a brawl going on behind me everywhere I went around the floor.

Ann performed with the popular Three Stooges.

hardly keep my composure. I didn't understand half of what they were saying, but it didn't matter. The joy they brought those sick kids was priceless. Afterward we went around and talked to all the kids. It felt so good. They passed out their pictures and gave me one, too. I chuckled to myself for days after.

Off stage they were polite, gentlemanly, and slightly reserved. I must say, they were very well dressed, too. I still can't believe I performed with the Three Stooges, and I never told anyone outside the Steel Pier because I didn't imagine anyone else would believe it either. I was their stooge for a good cause.

I still can't believe I performed with the Three Stooges, and I never told anyone outside the Steel Pier because I didn't imagine anyone else would believe it either.

11.
Travelin' Man

Throngs of teenyboppers swarmed onto the pier like bees to honey. They created havoc and many were taken away in ambulances. They fainted from heat, dehydration, and, in my opinion, pure hysteria.

One morning I got a phone call from Steel Pier owner George Hamid Jr. He said Ricky Nelson was going to land in a helicopter on the pier and I was to put on my bathing suit and welcome him. It was a photo op. Publicity for the pier, of course. I think I had fifteen or twenty minutes to throw myself together, and I did just that. I was a mess and I knew it.

Rick, as he liked to be called, was a well-dressed dreamboat, but he was so sweet and friendly! We talked a little as they took pictures, then security whisked him away. There were so many people on the pier to see Ricky Nelson that seven water shows were scheduled that day to accommodate the crowds.

Throngs of teenyboppers swarmed onto the pier like bees to honey. They created havoc and many were taken away in ambulances. They fainted from heat, dehydration, and, in my opinion, pure hysteria. There was not enough security to contain them, and we feared there would be a stampede. Getting through the crowd from the end of the pier was near impossible and took forever, so we started bringing food in the morning and staying on the pier for our dinner break—which was really not much of a break. With seven shows to do, they were almost back to back.

Rick performed in the ballroom not the theater. Thousands could stand in the ballroom and overflow to the outside, and stand they did, packed together like sardines in a can. All records for attendance were broken that day. There were 44,000 people on the pier to see Ricky Nelson.

There was a suite of dressing rooms above the ballroom for Rick and his band. His helicopter landed on the roof so he got on and off the pier with no problem. Rick and I sent messages back and forth to each other by Pat, the manager of the ballroom. Rick was sort of a prisoner in his suite. Rick's dressing room was just next to the diving horse area where I was, so he was really nearby. It made our fun and games easy. He would send Pat to see if I had some scissors he could borrow to trim his hair. I don't know what all else he asked for, but it was fun and funny. I was kind of a prisoner, too, because of all the extra shows.

Before he left that year, he asked me to exchange pictures and said we should stay in touch. We did stay in touch, and he sent me his long-playing albums with little notes. We continued this through the winter. Soon after Rick arrived on the pier the next year, Pat came back to see me. He told me Rick wanted to know if I would come to his dressing room. Pat said he would come back and take me upstairs to Rick's suite. Rick was asking for me. I was nervous.

Pat took me into his suite and Rick introduced me to his band (only three guys). He was so nice that I relaxed, and we found that we had lots in common. Rick was into doing trapeze work. So was I. We talked for a while. They played guitars and we drank Cokes. Rick took me into his room. We talked some more. We talked about music, about horses, about trapeze, and so forth. He held my hand. He had calluses on the ends of his fingers. I commented that I could see he was a serious musician because you don't get that from "picking a little." He said he didn't want to be one of the "white-teeth guys." I knew exactly what he meant. There were so many rock 'n' roll idols who came and went so fast in those days.

Rick's dressing room was just next to the diving horse area where I was, so he was really nearby. It made our fun and games easy. He would send Pat to see if I had some scissors he could borrow to trim his hair. I don't know what all else he asked for, but it was fun and funny.

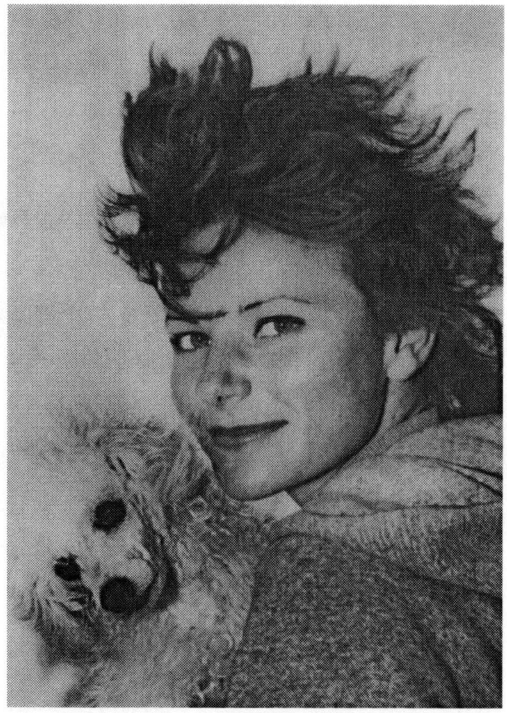

These are the pictures that Ricky Nelson and Ann Miles exchanged. Ann is holding her dog Cheri.

One or two hits—lots of white teeth and image and not much else. Rick was not one of those guys in any way and would go on to prove it, but it took years and some hard times to earn his Rock and Roll Hall of Fame induction.

Okay, I know what you're thinking. Did we have sex? Remember, this was the late 1950s, not the '60s yet. We weren't into drugs, and we didn't hop into bed with everyone at a moment's notice. Love was the thing back then. Meeting someone you were attracted to, dating, and looking forward to the next time you would see them, thinking about them when you were away from them, and wondering when or if they would call. This was fun and exciting. Little gifts in the mail, etc., and, yes, kissing and cuddling, but not a booty call! This was a sweet, exciting, hot little romance, but most of all I liked him as a person. The more I knew, the more I liked.

It didn't seem to bother him that girls tried to tear his clothes off everywhere he went. It scared the hell outta me. He had to have security to get him from place to place. At that time, he traveled a lot, and I got the idea he was lonely to just have a private life. He'd say, "By the time I'm twenty-one, I could be washed up." I knew that wouldn't happen, but I'm not so sure he did.

There would be more meetings, and Rick asked me to go to The 500 Club with him. That was a club in Atlantic City that featured big-name stars of the day, like Frank Sinatra. I saw Sammy Davis Jr. there, among others. This all just seemed surreal to me, even though I had met most of the rock 'n' roll heartthrobs of the day—Fabian, Frankie Avalon, Bobby Rydell, Bobby Darin, Conway Twitty, Chubby Checker, Paul Anka… The list goes on and on. Rick was different. There was a real connection between us. We shared some of the same interests, and talk came easy. He asked me to come to California. He said he'd show me the studio where he worked. I wanted to, but I guess I was just plain scared. Where would I stay, and how would I get there? What would I wear? What would his parents, Ozzie and Harriet, think? What would my parents think? I didn't say any of this to Rick. Maybe I should have. I was just a naive teenager out of the woods of Arkansas in the middle of the Fabulous Fifties. Rick was the undisputed teen idol of the day. He had already starred in *The Adventures of Ozzie and Harriet* for years and now was a pop/rock star at the top of the charts. Not to mention the feature films he appeared in… He was America's sweetheart and my sweetheart, too.

We were both 18 years old when we met. I was struggling to make enough money to stay in college. He was a millionaire. There was a sweetness about him and he was down-to-earth real. He never did anything that made me feel uncomfortable—all the opposite. Nevertheless, it was all a bit overwhelming. We stayed in touch for a few years, which wasn't so easy. I was all over the country; he was all over the world. Geography is hard to fight. Some of Rick's greatest hits were "Travelin' Man," "Hello Mary Lou," "My Bucket's Got a Hole in It," "Leaving It Up to You," "Fools Rush In," and "Garden Party." There were many more.

We were both 18 years old when we met. I was struggling to make enough money to stay in college. He was a millionaire. There was a sweetness about him and he was down-to-earth real. He never did anything that made me feel uncomfortable—all the opposite.

There were lots of celebrities who came back to visit through those years into the 1960s, most of them hanging out between their shows in the theater. They would see our show and then come back stage. Johnnie Ray was in Lorena's room all the time. He would take my arm (he was blind), and I would walk him around the end of the pier and tell him about the tower and the rigging and everything I could see. By that time, the horse had an elevator for his assent to the top. I still climbed a ladder.

This was before paparazzi were on the scene; everything was more casual. Big-name stars could actually mingle with the public and not worry about stalkers or tabloid assaults.

This was before paparazzi were on the scene; everything was more casual. Big-name stars could actually mingle with the public and not worry about stalkers or tabloid assaults.

12. Boardwalk Memories

There was a big storm in 1962 that washed away the end of the Steel Pier and took the horse tower and tank out to sea. They replaced it, putting an elevator in the horse tower and using a tank that was put together in pieces so the whole thing took up much less space.

In the fall I would go to Tallahassee, back to the books and gymnastics. Each summer I would return to Atlantic City and the horses. In and around Tallahassee, I would be at the beach or scuba diving in underwater caves in my free time. I even took to studying at the beach.

There was a big storm in 1962 that washed away the end of the Steel Pier and took the horse tower and tank out to sea. They replaced it, putting an elevator in the horse tower and using a tank that was put together in pieces so the whole thing took up much less space. It was no longer stationary, so it could travel. Now Hamid, the pier owner, started booking state fairs and other appearances for the diving horse after the season on the pier. I got permission from school to do these special appearances. Since it was my sole support, they allowed me to make up my class time.

When Memorial Day rolled around, I was on my way back to Atlantic City. I could hardly wait to get back. I'd even go a few days early and walk the boards. By this time, I knew people up and down the boardwalk—vendors that came back every year and workmen on the Steeplechase Pier that let me ride the rides for free. I loved the sound of seagulls and a calliope in the distance. The rolling chairs—like rickshaws but pushed instead of pulled—on the boardwalk were in constant motion. (The modernized versions ran on batteries.)

I'd take off my shoes and walk along the water's edge. The Globe burlesque theater was open for a midnight show. I talked the divers into taking me with them. That's where I saw Sally Rand and Virginia "Ding Dong" Bell. She had the biggest boobs I'd ever seen—and that's before implants! We always went backstage and talked to the comedians—and sometimes even a stripper or two. (Just look them in the eye when you talk to them and don't look down!) I saw Lucy the Elephant, which is an elephant-shaped hotel in Margate.

I sometimes went to dinner at Jim Fadigan's home. Jim was my friend from FSU who recommended me to Lorena for diving the horses. Jim was a diver on the pier. He had recommended two other girls, too, but I never saw or heard of them coming around. Dr. James Fadigan, PhD, is my dear friend to this day.

There was a midnight movie about a block down the boards from the Steel Pier where I saw *Psycho*. When I got back to the hotel after the movie, I went down the hall to the shower, but I couldn't do it. I had to wait until the next morning to take a shower.

When I went back to school I missed Atlantic City. I missed nights in my dressing room when the show got rained out. There was a beaver-board roof and a window looking out to sea. I would open my window and lie on my single bed looking out, with the sound of rain on the roof. Sometimes, Owen the stage hand would bring tea and we'd have tea and talk. He had been a vaudeville performer. He and his wife, June, were a dance team. These were the nights when there would always be a poker game in the divers' room. They shared a large room so would set up a table and play into the night. They invited everyone to play, but it wasn't for me. I didn't like cards much. I'd go to Lorena's room. We'd have coffee,

When I went back to school I missed Atlantic City. I missed nights in my dressing room when the show got rained out. There was a beaver-board roof and a window looking out to sea. I would open my window and lie on my single bed looking out, with the sound of rain on the roof.

and she talked about when she was little. Her father, Doc Carver the world-champion rifle shot, had a big knot on his hand from shooting so much. She said Buffalo Bill Cody taught her to read when she was small, and she sat on his knee. Since her father had a show with sharp shooters and a diving horse, she talked about touring around the country and staying in fancy hotels and paying with gold pieces. She said at that time they traveled in wagons. Some think that the expression "I'm on the wagon" or "I fell off the wagon" came from the fact that Buffalo Bill was a drinker, big time. The crew would watch him to see if he fell off the wagon. If he did, they knew they had to sober him up before the show. If he stayed on the wagon, everything was okay.

After her father died, Lorena continued to tour the country with the diving horse act. Later she came to the Steel Pier, where she stayed until the mid-1970s. We became close friends, and I stayed in touch with her until her death in 1981.

After the pier season one year, Lorena and I drove to Barton, Vermont, where I rode in the Topsfield Fair. After every show, people would come up to me and say they had seen Lorena ride there in the '20s and never forgot it. I didn't dive into a tank there. They dug a hole and the fire department filled it with water. I dove into it like Lorena used to do.

I told Lorena I was always in trouble when I was a kid. I was drawn to daredevil feats and would fall out of a tree into Mother's flowerbed and smash the daffodils or something. I got many whippings. (They used to do that, you know.) After my whipping, Mother always told me to sit down, shut up, and be nice! I couldn't, though; I was learning my stunts.

I got many whippings. (They used to do that, you know.) After my whipping, Mother always told me to sit down, shut up, and be nice! I couldn't, though; I was learning my stunts.

13.

Dangerous Waters

The tank I had on the pier before the storm was very heavy and was riveted together—not suitable for travel and too heavy to transport. The new tank was bolted together and made of aluminum or some lighter-weight metal.

George Hamid Sr. owned the New Jersey State Fair and the Hamid-Morton Circus, among other things. After the horse tower had an elevator for the horse and Hamid had a tower and tank built for traveling, he wanted to do state fairs and other appearances after the Steel Pier season closed each year. He also wanted to put the diving horse in the Hamid-Morton Circus. I suspect this was the real reason for building that type of tower/tank. The tower was now metal and could be taken apart for travel. It could be loaded onto a truck in pieces. The tank I had on the pier before the storm was very heavy and was riveted together—not suitable for travel and too heavy to transport. The new tank was bolted together and made of aluminum or some lighter-weight metal. It could be taken apart and loaded on a truck in parts, and it could be set up indoors. The tower was like the one I had on the pier.

Hamid had this new tank and tower set up on the outskirts of Atlantic City. They built a ramp and a platform for the horse to exit. He had me go out early one morning to test this new set up. I think he could have done this without a rider—I only weighed 105 pounds. My being there would have made little if any difference, but he said he wanted my opinion.

The next year when I came back for the pier season, people (crew guys, divers, etc.) rushed up and hugged me. They told me they were glad to see me. I didn't know what this was all about until they showed me a news clipping and told me the bad news.

I did a couple of dives with the horse and it seemed all right, but I thought the tank was a little flimsy and maybe shifted slightly on impact. Thankfully, it held together and weathered the test.

I told him that I didn't like the fact that the tower was guyed to the tank because if the tank didn't hold up, it would take the tower down. He said he would reinforce the tank with steel cables around the outside. He asked if I would be interested in riding in the circus after the pier season each year. I said I would have to give it some thought. I was still in school and couldn't afford to lose that much school time, but I told him that I might do a state fair or other appearance that was not for an extended period of time.

I did think about it over the next week or so. Something bothered me about that tank, though. I just had an uneasy feeling about it. I was not interested in being on the road, and I also didn't trust just anybody to put things together. I wouldn't have my own crew that was there permanently like on the pier. I feared they would hire people who weren't so careful or knowledgeable. The bottom line was I didn't want to interrupt my college education and didn't want to travel with the circus. I turned it down.

He did put it in the circus. He hired some of the divers from the pier to go. They would dive off the horse tower as a lead up to the diving horse. Apparently they got a girl to ride the horse.

At any rate, the next year when I came back for the pier season, people (crew guys, divers, etc.) rushed up and hugged me. They told me they were glad to see me. I didn't know what this was all about until they showed me a news clipping and told me the bad news: Sure enough, the tank had burst. Even with steel cables around it. As I had feared, it took down the tower. When it came down, there were divers on the tower and one diver in midair with another climbing the tower. Live electrical wires were in the water on the floor. Three divers were injured. It was serious, and the horse would have been up next.

One of my favorite divers, Athos Darigo, suffered fractures of the left leg and right arm. Gary Gains suffered a back injury. Hartley French suffered chest and rib injuries. I didn't know Gains or French. It seems the tank had collapsed from the bottom and pulled the bottom of the tower. It fell into the arena, not into the audience. Thank God! I read the article over and over again.

Athos said they were climbing up the tower when they heard a big noise. The tower started leaning. Athos fell about 20 feet, then the tower fell on his ankle. Gains was diving. He heard the tank break as he was falling toward it. Usually it had about ten feet of water in it. It had maybe five feet of water when he hit. By the time he stood up, most of it was gone. Then he was struck in the back by a falling object. French was on the diving board and tried to climb down. He climbed part of the way down then jumped about ten feet. Water knocked him down, and the tower fell across his back. Riggers rescued the two divers trapped under the tower. They were all taken to the hospital. Lucky to be alive, I guess.

I felt so bad for them. At the same time, I was grateful I listened to my gut feeling about the tank. These things do happen sometimes, even if you are careful.

I did a few fairs off season, with a hole dug in the ground and the fire department filling it with water. This is the way they always used to do it in the old days. That was fine with me! The hole had an incline on one end for the horse to climb out. A heavy liner was placed in the hole before it was filled with water. No problem. Bags of sawdust are placed over the liner to cushion it for the horse and to hold the liner in place. New ways aren't always better! This experience taught me that you should always listen to your gut feelings. This is your inner voice coming from a higher power.

It seems the tank had collapsed from the bottom and pulled the bottom of the tower. It fell into the arena, not into the audience. Thank God! I read the article over and over again.

Coming into Manhattan for the first time to stay took my breath away. I got out of the train at Penn Station with my one suitcase and checked into the Penn Terminal Hotel on 34th Street. I went directly to Macy's department store and applied for a job. Any job!

14. The Big Apple

George Hamid Jr. would sometimes send me to New York City to do publicity for the Steel Pier. I was on *What's My Line?*, *To Tell the Truth*, and *Who Do You Trust?* with host Johnny Carson—all kinds of radio and TV shows. I met many celebrities there. I was taken to a Broadway show by Bill Doll and his wife. He was the publicity agent for the pier. I sat next to Lauren Bacall to see *The Music Man* starring Robert Preston.

I was always glad to get back to the pier. New York City was a little scary to me. I wanted to go back, though. I wanted to be in a Broadway show and, after all, I majored in dance, so where else would I go? I went to New York! I didn't go back to school, even though I lacked only a few credits to graduate. I went to NYC with very little money and no idea what life in Manhattan would cost—I mean financially, emotionally, physically, in every way.

Coming into Manhattan for the first time to stay took my breath away. I got out of the train at Penn Station with my one suitcase and checked into the Penn Terminal Hotel on 34th Street. I went directly to Macy's department store and applied for a job. Any job! I ended up at the perfume counter a few months before

Christmas. People were already shopping for Christmas gifts and fragrance was high on their list.

I made enough money to pay my hotel bill and have one hamburger a day. At Thanksgiving that year, I sprang for a rotisserie chicken. The next day, broke and hungry, I dug the chicken bones out of the wastebasket and that was my food for the day. In those days, Times Square was not only the theater district but the porn theater district, too. Prostitutes roamed the streets freely. I came home smelling of every perfume I had demonstrated all day, so I was probably frequently mistaken for a hooker. The Penn Terminal Hotel wasn't the best place to live for keeping up appearances.

It was a low point in my life. My parents kept nagging me to come home. A suitor from FSU came to New York pressuring me to marry him. I had already said no, but he kept coming on. I finally succumbed, and we got a small apartment in Brooklyn. I traveled into Manhattan on the subway every day to my job at Macy's.

We were just scraping by. I had no warm clothes and no boots. It was one of the coldest winters that year. Once, it snowed so bad the elevated subways didn't run from Brooklyn and Macy's closed for a day. Unheard of! My one pair of heels didn't survive. I went to a thrift store and bought a warm jacket and boots for myself.

At this point, I knew if I was to survive in Manhattan, I needed to find a better way. I was so depressed I could hardly function. My marriage was a failure. I went home to Arkansas for three months and filed for divorce.

It was a low point in my life. My parents kept nagging me to come home. A suitor from FSU came to New York pressuring me to marry him. I had already said no, but he kept coming on. I finally succumbed, and we got a small apartment in Brooklyn.

15. Playboy Bunny

We were measured for custom-made outfits and sent to the ob-gyn for exams. We had to get a cabaret license to work—maybe that was part of it. I think they just wanted to know we were healthy and free of disease.

I was out of school, so what I needed now was a career. Even more to the point, I needed a job.

It was the mid-1960s and everything was changing. It wasn't just my life that was in upheaval, it was the whole country and everything in it, so it seemed to me. Women burned their bras. Men burned their draft cards. Blacks burned Los Angeles. Hugh Hefner opened his Playboy clubs all over the country. The closest one to me was in New Orleans, so that's where I went. I applied for a position as a Playboy Bunny.

There were hundreds of girls applying, and I met a woman who lived in New Orleans. She had an extra room she rented to me until I knew what my outcome would be. We were both accepted to work. We met the Bunny Mother, a young, attractive blonde who, as it happened, was Hefner's secretary when he first started *Playboy* magazine. She advised us on everything and was sort of like the housemother we had in college.

We were measured for custom-made outfits and sent to the ob-gyn for exams. We had to get a cabaret license to work—maybe that was part of it. I think they just wanted to know we were healthy and free of disease.

We then began a training program where we learned the "bunny dip." It was a way of approaching the table in which you braced your thigh against the table and bent backwards to serve drinks. This way you didn't have your boobs in anyone's face. They were on display enough as it was, I guess. We had to fill out our checks a certain way so that we called the member's name and served him first. The order was written clockwise on the check so you always served the right person the correct drink. Bar orders were called a certain way so everyone called the same way, and bartenders placed orders on your tray as they were to be served. In our training period we learned names of drinks and how they were made. Cocktails were mixed at the table, but you had to ask, "May I mix for you?"

"Bunny Annie" on the job at a Playboy Club in New Orleans.

It was fairly dark in the club, so we had a small flashlight that hung on the string that laced up the side of our costume. There was a small ledge of fabric under the inside bust of our costume for holding tips. As the night wore on, the bigger your tips, the bigger your boobs. My ambition was to be Fort Knox on Heels by dinner time. The trick was to get your boobs higher than your hair. In those days that was pretty high the popular hairstyle of the day was the beehive.

You were not allowed to see customers outside the club, and they hired Pinkerton detectives to make sure you didn't. They would pose as customers and try to make dates with you, then hand in written reports to management on your reaction.

There was one customer you could go out with, however—a local restaurateur who invited several girls at a time to have dinner at one of his restaurants. You got a written invitation approved by management and went in a group at his expense. It was quite nice. In fact, everything about our employment at the club was quite nice. There were floor managers that made sure everything was above board. Customers weren't allowed to touch us or bother us in any way. We were not allowed to be anything but polite and businesslike. We were Bunnies, not Playmates! That was a whole other thing.

There were floor managers that made sure everything was above board. Customers weren't allowed to touch us or bother us in any way. We were not allowed to be anything but polite and businesslike. We were Bunnies, not Playmates! That was a whole other thing.

Most of the Bunnies were like me, just trying to make a living. I needed to get back to Atlantic City, then to New York City. That would take some money. Several of the other girls were divorced with a couple of kids to support. We were glorified cocktail waitresses but making more money than other waitresses—LOTS MORE! I worked extra hours when I could. I worked as many hours as my feet would take. We had to wear three-inch heels on a tile floor in the Playmate bar carrying a tray full of drinks all night. There was a fountain in the New Orleans club. It was the only place you could sit if you weren't busy, which was seldom. If you did sit, you couldn't just sit—you had to pose, really. The system was flawless.

When they thought you were good enough, you would be promoted to work the showrooms upstairs where big-name stars, singers, comedians, etc., performed. It was supposed to be a chance to make more money, as there would be two or three shows a night. The showrooms were small and would fill quickly. You took drink orders and for those who wanted to eat, there was a buffet that served steaks. You sold passes shaped like a key for food, and the tab added up quick and steep. So did your tips. After the show, the room emptied quickly, and then you did it all over again. It was dark and crowded, and I didn't like it so much. After a while, I requested to go back to the Playmate bar. You could actually get to know your customers there. They came back frequently and would ask for you by name. I was Bunny Annie. I had quite a few regulars, and I tried to make sure they always had a good time. I learned all the members' names and did my best to please them—maybe to a fault in one instance…

I was Bunny Annie. I had quite a few regulars, and I tried to make sure they always had a good time. I learned all the members' names and did my best to please them.

This is a Bunny tale about Bunny tails. As you may know, Bunnies wore fluffy, round, white tails strategically placed on the backs of their costumes. It was attached with hooks and eyes, and it lifted off easily when the costume went to the cleaner. These tails, along with other souvenirs, were sold in the gift shop. Some customers, however, wanted the tail of their favorite Bunny. They would ask you to give them your tail or offer to buy it from you. I always directed them to the gift shop, but it became a running joke. They thought my tail was bigger, fluffier, and prettier than the ones in the gift shop. It really was, too, because (thanks to my Maw Maw) I knew how to make them and I made my own tails. Finally, I made a few extras and when the subject came up again I said, "I can't give you my tail. I would be in big trouble for that, but if I was busy serving drinks and it got 'lifted,' I wouldn't know, would I? Whoever did that would have to get it out of sight in a hurry and be careful that a floor manager wouldn't see." They loved it! It became a game. They had so much fun I had to stop. It caused too much commotion. I had to go to the locker room to replace my tail. It was fun while it lasted, but, alas, it was not the thing to do. Too risky for me.

I usually had a bite to eat at the local hangout after work. It was a small tavern about a block from the club. There was a jukebox that played all night. We danced and had the best burger in town. I rented a studio apartment upstairs. I had met the owner of the building, who owned and ran the bar. Nothing fancy for sure,

One day a delivery truck pulled up in front of my apartment and before I knew it, boxes and boxes were delivered to my door. They were addressed to me. They had my name on them, so I took them. Inside were towels, sheets, tablecloths, and napkins.

but it was near work and my dog was welcome. I had a toy poodle that always traveled with me. She had gotten distemper and was so ill I thought she wouldn't make it. She tried to follow me around when she couldn't even walk, so I took to carrying her and feeding her by hand. She did get well. The vet couldn't believe it.

I found it hard to make friends in New Orleans. Everyone seemed to have problems. They were alcoholics or divorced with several children or just looking for sex, into drugs, etc. You name it, it was all there.

One day a delivery truck pulled up in front of my apartment and before I knew it, boxes and boxes were delivered to my door. They were addressed to me. They had my name on them, so I took them. Inside were towels, sheets, tablecloths, and napkins. There was enough linen to service a hotel. Well, that's a little bit of a stretch but not much. This gift came from a man I'd met in the bar downstairs through my landlord. It seemed he wanted to date me, and he asked my landlord what kind of gift he could get me. My landlord told him I had just moved in and probably needed things for the apartment.

Long story short—I dated this man for a short time. He took me to lunch and dinner at every nice or well-known restaurant in New Orleans. Later, he would take me to his motel residence, where I could swim in the pool. Dinner there was with some of his business associates. After dinner I was given rolls of quarters to go to the pay phone and call my family and friends so I would be out of the way and they could talk business. One time before he took me home, we stopped in a large room full of phones with people on every one of them. I was secretly alarmed at this and beginning to suspect he was not on the up and up when I spotted a newspaper article. He was in New Orleans on trial. It seems he was not a small-time gangster but someone Bobby Kennedy was out to get. He was a big-time sports bookie and tax evader—and maybe was involved with drugs.

I had been wanting to leave New Orleans and get back to Manhattan. This was the incentive I needed. I went into the club early the next day. In the office, I gave my notice, but when the manager heard I wanted to go to NYC, he had an offer to make. He said they had been considering having a hostess in the Manhattan club who would sign new members at a desk near the entrance. If I was interested, they would transfer me there and create the position for me. Not only was I interested, I was grateful! It would solve my problem of getting a job in Manhattan and mean I could probably afford to get an apartment there. I could tell my gangster-friend, "Sorry, gotta go!" We worked out the details, like salary and when I would start work, and they even paid my airfare.

On my way back to NYC, I visited my family in Arkansas. My little dog, Cheri, was getting older and her illness had left her having little "fits." She needed a stable home. Mother took good care of her for many years to come.

I had been wanting to leave New Orleans and get back to Manhattan. This was the incentive I needed. I went into the club early the next day. In the office, I gave my notice, but when the manager heard I wanted to go to NYC, he had an offer to make.

I fell in love with Manhattan the first time I arrived there, but it didn't fall in love with me right away. I talked funny, and people couldn't believe how naïve and innocent I was.

16. Show Biz

I fell in love with Manhattan the first time I arrived there, but it didn't fall in love with me right away. I talked funny, and people couldn't believe how naïve and innocent I was. I couldn't wear my jeans to job interviews, and I didn't really know how to dress any other way. I wasn't sophisticated. My taste was pretty tacky. Good thing I had a job where I wore a uniform. The Manhattan Playboy Club put a large desk in the Playmate bar, where I greeted people and signed new members. My job included going to every floor each night and getting a tab average, so I got to know a lot of people who worked there. I wore a Playboy sweater, a skirt, and heels. No more skimpy outfit. I worked on a straight salary and was sitting at my desk most of the night.

I had gotten a not-so-cheap, not-so-expensive apartment in a not-so-good, not-so-bad neighborhood. It was on 48th Street, between Fifth and Sixth Avenues, right across from the "30 Rock" building. It was not a residential area, but there were apartments there—walk-ups above the stores. Later I found out it was pretty safe as New York apartments go because Rockefeller Center had security people who patrolled the area in cars. My neighbor across the hall and I became friends. She told me about security. There was another girl upstairs we were friends with, too. I was beginning to feel at home here, finally.

My new job at Playboy didn't leave me dead tired like being a Bunny had. I started thinking about why I was in Manhattan. I wanted a career in show business. I wanted to dance in shows and study acting. When I was young, I used to say I wanted to ride horses and be in the movies. I have always loved movies. I still do. Horses, too, of course.

I started going to dance auditions during the day. The trade papers were full of ads, but I could only go to the non-union auditions. They were known as cattle calls and that's what they felt like. For Actors' Equity Association (AEA) union jobs, you had to have a union card to audition, but you couldn't get a card until you had a job. Mission Impossible!

I started going to dance auditions during the day. The trade papers were full of ads. but I could only go to the non-union auditions. They were known as cattle calls and that's what they felt like.

One day there was an ad in the trades for the national tour of *Carnival*. They were auditioning dancers but also looking for someone who could do Spanish Web. I could do that! Spanish Web is the rope you see girls in the circus hanging from by a foot loop or hand loop performing acrobatic tricks as a web sitter spins the rope from below. It was a union audition, but I had no union card. I went anyway. As I suspected, there were dancers galore but not many who would go on the web.

The director and choreographer were there. I explained to the assistant choreographer that I was non-union but that I had experience on the web and that I was a dancer. They auditioned me and I got the job. Not only did I get my AEA card, but since I did a specialty spot on the web, I was a principal. That meant more money and a more prestigious union card. With an Actors' Equity card that listed me as a principal, I could now audition as a dancer and as a principal actor. WOW! That fall and all winter, we toured the country with *Carnival*. I never worked so hard or had so much fun. I danced in the chorus and had a principal spot on the web.

Ann Blyth was the lead, and she was funny and fun. A real sport, too. She was very friendly, and she used to come into the chorus dressing room and shoot the breeze. She was known to tell an off-color joke occasionally. I still see some of the principal actors from that show on TV and in movies now. A couple of years later, I did *Carnival* again with Liza Minnelli. I danced and did my spot on the web again.

I still went to Atlantic City every summer to ride the horses. It was like a vacation on the Jersey shore now. Back in Manhattan, I had gotten a Dentyne chewing gum commercial on the trampoline. This was a different union. Now I had my Screen Actors Guild (SAG) card, which meant I could audition for movies as well as commercials. I had no steady job, and having union cards and going to auditions didn't mean you would work.

I needed an agent. To get an appointment was another catch-22. I started sending pictures and résumés to every agent in town. Unfortunately, I only had a few credits, so I got no response. You know—don't call us, we'll call you. I had gotten a few good jobs on my own, so I continued to try that. When things got rough, I would get a night job cocktail waitressing to pay rent. I kept at it and started getting more commercials. They paid residuals, so if your commercial ran, you could live on it for a while. I once had seven class-A principal, on-camera commercials running at the same time. I also discovered print work (still photography). They hired models for products. I was perfect for demonstrating exercise equipment, etc.

I needed an agent. To get an appointment was another catch-22. I started sending pictures and résumés to every agent in town. Unfortunately, I only had a few credits, so I got no response. You know—don't call us, we'll call you.

I made rounds every day I wasn't working. I would go to agents, photographers, and ad agencies, always checking the union bulletin boards—anything I could think of—and I would leave a picture and résumé. Now I had more credits. But still no response from agents.

17.
Stuntgirl

Stuntman Peter Hock and I worked for Allen Funt regularly on Candid Camera. I don't know if all these shows aired, but he kept us busy. He was always dreaming up some crazy scheme to draw unsuspecting people in.

I got a call for a movie stunt. This job led to more stunt work, and there were lots of movies and TV shows filming in New York City. Directors called me. I had met the busy stuntmen, and they would call me. Alex Stevens was the top stunt coordinator. I worked for him more and more now. I had found my niche and was getting a reputation as a stuntgirl. I did high falls, stair falls, and fire and water stunts. I did a little (very little) stunt driving and chases over roof tops, etc. Just about anything they could think of, I did. Once I went hand-over-hand on a rope from boat to shore. I was set on fire many times, and one of the scariest things I did was crash a car into the water. In one movie, I was supposedly burned to death in a whole set that was burning.

Stuntman Peter Hock and I worked for Allen Funt regularly on *Candid Camera*. I don't know if all these shows aired, but he kept us busy. He was always dreaming up some crazy scheme to draw unsuspecting people in. He kept us working, and he was running the show. He had us fall through a false ceiling, had us fight each other, etc. We would do this over and over all day long. It got so I hated for him to call. I knew I would come home beat up.

In those days there were no air bags, so we did high falls into cardboard boxes. We cut the corners off so when you hit, it broke your fall and then the boxes deflated and let you down easy. Well, fairly easy. My FSU gymnastics training made high falls pretty easy for me. It was just an extension of my work on the trampoline and the teeter board. Instead of being caught by someone, I landed in a way that my weight was solid and distributed evenly.

For fire stunts, we didn't wear fire suits. Instead, we prepared an under-dress with foil and a wet wrap like a mummy. Wardrobe went on top of that, and we made the wardrobe damp. We didn't really have any protection for our face and hair. Most times I wore a wig, which was even more dangerous because when a wig caught fire, it melted and stuck to you. Glue was smeared on over the damp wardrobe so hopefully the glue burned instead of our clothes or us. A few years after I started doing stunt work, a guy named Gary Zeller invented a substance you could coat your skin with and it would burn for a minute or two and not burn your skin. He called it Zel-Jel. I used it on my face and hands from then on. Sometimes I put it on my hair under a wig. I think he got an Oscar for that invention. There is a separate category for the science part of arts and sciences; it is not a televised event.

For fire stunts, we didn't wear fire suits. Instead, we prepared an under-dress with foil and a wet wrap like a mummy. Wardrobe went on top of that, and we made the wardrobe damp. We didn't really have any protection for our face and hair.

I did horseback stunts, too, like commercials on a jumping horse and a Hai Karate fragrance commercial as a jockey with comedian David Brenner. I did a couple of *McCloud* episodes riding a runaway horse in Central Park.

Early on in my career, I had gotten a job to do a stair fall. This was easy for me. I had special thin, hard rubber pads that I made for myself. I taped them on with duct tape where I needed them. The guys all wore football pads, knee pads, etc. Since there weren't football pads to fit me, and if I wore them I looked like a man, I devised my own way of working. I liked to be free to move easily, so I used thin pads with Ace bandages and tape. You couldn't even tell they were there when the clothes were on. I could carry everything I needed in a small shoulder bag.

I had an early afternoon call on this job, and I went to an interview for a modeling job that morning. I came still dressed from my interview. BIG MISTAKE! I checked in and met the director. The assistant director showed me to the stairwell where my stunt was to be shot. They were still shooting another scene. He told me I could take a look at the stairs and then they would come get me for make-up and hair when they were near my shot. An hour went by and a man came into the hallway. I asked if he was taking me to make-up. He said, no, he was an actor, and he sat down on the steps and started talking to me. He said, "What do you think?" I said the stairs are marble, so they are worse than wood, and there are lots of them but that was okay.

I had an early afternoon call on this job, and I went to an interview for a modeling job that morning. I came still dressed from my interview. BIG MISTAKE!

He asked if I had pads and gear I needed and so on. I said I did. I said I didn't need much, just in the right places. I had done many stair falls. He said, "Do you always dress like that?" I thought that was a strange thing to ask. Then he told me he had overheard the director talking to the cameraman and script person to cut the stunt scene. He said, "They don't think you can do it. You don't look like a stunt person. I just wanted to give you a heads-up." That man was Peter Falk before *Columbo*. Bless him! Sure enough, almost another hour went by and then the assistant director came into the hallway and told me they were running way behind and wouldn't be able to get to the stunt that day, so they cut it. He thanked me very much and said I would be paid for my time. I felt so stupid and humiliated that I went home and cried. From that day forward, when I went to a stunt job, I carried a large bag whether I needed it or not and wore jeans. Likewise, when I went to a modeling interview, I didn't let it be known that I was a stuntgirl. They might be afraid I would come in bruised or cut or something. I wanted to do both, so I kept them separate.

This will probably sound crazy to most normal people, but, for me, stunt work was a relief from anxiety. I have always had free-floating anxiety. It was social anxiety about not being good enough, about money or the lack of it, about not being validated, about not being approved of. I had no support growing up, but I had guts. Stunt work seemed tailor made for me and I for it. I was drawn to daredevil feats even as a child. I came alive learning. I had a God-given feel for it. I honed it to the max. It gave me confidence and made me happy. It was the place where, rather than being scared or anxious, I became totally liberated. I was so concentrated and laser focused I lived only in the moment. For me, that is freedom from anxiety. I'm not saying there was not some fear, but it was only in gray areas or when I was learning something new.

However, a little fear helps you stay focused and avoid injury. Maybe I was an adrenalin junkie? If I was self-medicating, I can't think of a better way to do it. A large amount of fear is debilitating. A little fear puts your hormones in the right place to work for you. It feels more like excitement. Almost like falling in love. I fell in love with stunt work.

A large amount of fear is debilitating. A little fear puts your hormones in the right place to work for you. It feels more like excitement. Almost like falling in love. I fell in love with stunt work.

It took two or three years for me to get to the point where I had enough credits on my résumé and my pictures were good enough for an agent to interview me. In the meantime, I was more experienced and felt really solid in my work. Not every stunt is an over-the-top thriller. There were a lot of stair falls, chases, karate-type fights, and falls out of speed boats. There were also falls from first-, second-, and third-story windows. There were runaway horse scenes and chases over the roof or in the rafters of a theater. There were fire and water stunts, too. I felt lucky because I always had something different going on in my work. When I asked my friends what they did that day they usually said—same ol', same ol'. If I didn't do a stunt that day, I would be doing a commercial on the trampoline or something. When they asked me, I would say I jumped out a third-story window or got set on fire or something along those lines.

Maybe you would like to know what it is like to get set on fire. This is one of the stunts in which fear is present—and it had better be. Fire is dangerous! By the time you realize something is wrong, it's too late. It is probably one of the few stunts that is taken seriously by almost everyone. There are some smaller fire stunts that don't get as much attention, but still there is usually a firefighter on set. I will tell you about one that is bigger. This is one where the whole set is on fire and so are you. In this case, there are more like four or five firefighters on set. Extinguishers and other equipment are plentiful and in plain sight all around. There are actors in the scene dressed like firefighters, but you can tell pretty quick who is and who is not a real one. Not all stunts have a stunt coordinator, but this kind of stunt always does—and in this case there was a fire and explosives expert as well. His name was Stash. He wore a patch on one eye, as his eye had been lost years earlier in an explosive stunt. Stash was confident and relaxed. He knew exactly what he was doing and how to do it. He prepared the set first and left his crew there. The rest of the time after that he stuck by me. He watched me as my stunt coordinator helped me under-dress for the stunt. He wanted to know how I was prepared—I mean from the skin out.

Fire is dangerous! By the time you realize something is wrong, it's too late. It is probably one of the few stunts that is taken seriously by almost everyone.

How? Over cotton bikini and underwear. No more synthetics than you can help. Then spray your whole body with water. Over that you cover your whole body with aluminum foil—and don't be stingy! This repels the heat from the fire on your body. Over this goes cotton bandage strips. Wrap yourself like a mummy. Not too tight, so you can still move, and not too loose, so it stays in place. Now comes your wardrobe. Spray it with water on the inside until it is damp. After your clothes are on, spray them with water until they're damp on the outside.

Now Stash works his magic with rubber cement glue. Not just a little but handfuls. He knows just how much glue to smear on and where to put it so that the flames won't reach your face or hair if it can be helped. How you move can affect that, too.

The set is ignited and suddenly you realize this is for real! No wonder the fire department is here.

Now Stash is talking to me. He says, "I hope you got your money because this is going to look great! Don't worry, I will be with you every second. My crew will take care of the set so I can stick with you. If anything goes wrong—speak to me. Don't listen to anyone but me. I won't listen to anyone but you. I know your action is to come across the burning room and try to get the door open to go out. It will not open, and finally you sink to the floor and pass out. There will be flames all around you. Don't worry, don't rush, and don't panic. You will be fine. Take your time and do your action. After the director calls cut, I will put you out."

"Are you ready?" I say, "Yes—" He lights me with a lighter and there is a big whooshing sound, like a gas burner makes, only it was all around me. Wow! Adrenaline on steroids. The director calls action, and I walk into the burning set with burning boards falling near me to the door that I would try to open. I am in the middle of flames all around. I am a flaming torch. I don't feel a thing. Not even warm. I fight to try and get the door open until the director says, "You're feeling faint now. Slide down the door and pass out on the floor."

It seemed to me that I was lying on the floor for quite a while before he said "cut." As soon as he said it, Stash was on it. It only took a few minutes with the extinguisher. This fire stunt made every other fire stunt I did seem like nothing much.

"Are you ready?" I say. "Yes—" He lights me with a lighter and there is a big whooshing sound. like a gas burner makes. only it was all around me. Wow! Adrenaline on steroids.

18.
Imprints

I guess there are some who think stunt people are always anxious or scared when they are about to do a stunt, but that's not true. Some stunt people have a specialty—for instance, stunt driving or airplane stunts. Some only do high falls or maybe horseback stunts. These people are very good at their specialty and may have a job that requires them to do it every day, so they are always in practice. When a stunt job comes up, they take time off and do the stunt.

Then you have a group of stunt people who do a variety of stunts. They can be stunt coordinators or just do stunts full time. I did a variety of stunts that were more or less related and came under a category such as acrobatic, athletic, equestrian, and so forth. I also did commercial modeling and acting. At first glance, these things may not seem to be related, but believe me they are.

The skills you learn in gymnastics, high diving, and trampoline are the same skills you incorporate into doing a high fall, stair fall, and so forth. In the process of learning tricks, you also learn how to fall. Your mind is making an imprint of these skills for you—in your unconscious mind. You can't see it. You don't know where it is. You can't "call it up" at will or even know when or if it will ap-

The skills you learn in gymnastics, high diving, and trampoline are the same skills you incorporate into doing a high fall, stair fall, and so forth. In the process of learning tricks, you also learn how to fall.

pear. It is now a secret in your unconscious mind. When it does appear, athletes call it being in "the zone." Actors might call it the magic cocoon. Everything is effortless. You feel as if you can do no wrong. You just get out of the way and let your mind take over. The feeling is sublime!

Everything is effortless. You feel as if you can do no wrong. You just get out of the way and let your mind take over. The feeling is sublime!

Mind you, you don't get these imprints casually or without a lot of effort. It takes many hours and many years of hard work in the gym or wherever you learn your skills. Once the imprint is there, it becomes automatic. You have the "how" inside you. You are NOT scared because your conscious mind knows your unconscious mind knows "HOW."

19.

Agent Interviews

After my agent interviews, I hit a new low. They were brutal with their criticisms. I always needed to lose ten pounds. My hair was a mess; I would have to apply make-up and get a new wardrobe. My pictures were all wrong. To hear them tell it, there was nothing right about me. I did have quite a few good credits by now, though. I thought that would mean something. I guess that was the only reason they saw me at all.

No agent wanted to sign me because they said I was too specialized and I wasn't an experienced actor. Because I had a southern accent, they said they couldn't send me to auditions with lines. At that time, standard American speech was all that was acceptable. I hired a speech therapist and worked every day on a tape recorder to lose my accent. I went to the American Academy of Dramatic Arts and Strasberg Institute to study acting, then three years with Bobby Lewis, one of the founders of the Actors Studio. I did get a few acting parts but not enough to live on.

No agent wanted to sign me because they said I was too specialized and I wasn't an experienced actor. Because I had a southern accent, they said they couldn't send me to auditions with lines. At that time, standard American speech was all that was acceptable.

I kept working on my own to get commercials and stunt work, and I was getting a lot of print work now, too. Modeling (print work) was a pleasure for me. It wasn't something I had to spend years preparing for. It just grew out of my other work. It came about largely because I was photogenic, something I had nothing to do with. It wasn't physically taxing like stunt work where, frequently, I had to be prepared to make a considerable physical effort. Some of my product modeling involved things that required physical ability or sports, but there was as much or more that didn't. It was a place for me to relax and be pampered.

Most jobs took place in a photographer's studio in Manhattan, so I didn't have to travel to a location outside the city. There was always a make-up artist and a

Photos for modeling jobs, including one shot in the Virgin Islands with local children (lower right).

"5th Avenue" candy bars rained down on Ann during the making of this commercial.

hairdresser on set for me. I could roll out of bed, put on my sunglasses, and go. Once there, the client was nice to me and always knew my name. They were very considerate and respectful to me. It was good for my self-esteem and my ego.

In the hour or two while my make-up and hair were being done, the photographer would usually bring me coffee and a roll or something and sit down and talk about what he wanted to go for in the shoot. If there were products involved, they would give me a box full to take home.

Zooming through a supermarket on a skateboard for a soft-drink commercial.

I quit trying to get an agent to sign me and kept working on my own and through agents when they called me.

One of my favorite clients was the Virgin Islands Tourist Commission. Every year in February, the coldest time of year in New York City, I would go to the U.S. Virgin Islands to work for a week on the beaches and in hotels, then they paid my expenses to stay another week for vacation. I looked forward to it every year for a few years.

My acting classes, however, were a big disappointment to me. I was self-conscious and couldn't open up until I was accepted to study with Bobby Lewis. It was like a light came on and it all made sense to me, but I think it was a little too late. I was weary of starting from scratch and discouraged that I couldn't get an agent to sign me. My accent was a problem I never quite overcame.

Thankfully, all my hard work to this point was starting to pay off. I quit trying to get an agent to sign me and kept working on my own and through agents when they called me. They called often now. I was stunting regularly on soaps in addition to movies and commercials. There were print jobs, too. When there was a

Ann tied herself in a knot in this commercial for a stomach remedy.

Ann and her partner being filmed in a stunt for a pantyhose commercial.

commercial that had anything to do with trampoline, trapeze, skateboard, or acrobatics, agents would call me. I went for the one who called first. As it turned out, I got to know all the top agents. They negotiated my contracts, and I started making more money. Also, I learned I was a good commercial type. It was "the Pepsi generation" and I was in demand. I did Coke commercials, too. Coke and Pepsi were at war, competing in commercials. I was working almost every day. I couldn't afford to go back to the Steel Pier; I was too busy in Manhattan. I was happy with stunt work and commercial modeling, but I wasn't so confident about acting and I struggled with my speech. Speech therapy became less about acting and more about my personal healing. By this time, I was the busiest stunt person in NYC and one of the top commercial models. I let the acting go.

On weekends, I did a nightclub act with a fellow I met on the Steel Pier, Hugo Domenech. He came to the pier every year performing with his partner, Jose, but came back to the water show

Hugo and his wife, Cynthia, and their daughter lived in Queens. I would go there or he would come to Manhattan, and we worked on our hand-balancing act.

Another photo from her portfolio. Ann became one of the busiest stunt performers in New York City and one of the top commercial models.

on his dinner break and we worked out together. I met his wife and baby girl when they came to visit Atlantic City. He gave me his phone number in NYC, and I had gotten in touch with him. I became friends with his family. Hugo and his wife, Cynthia, and their daughter lived in Queens. I would go there or he would come to Manhattan, and we worked on our hand-balancing act. His partner, Jose, was gone by now and Hugo was starting to work in films as a grip (stagehand). He wanted to do that during the week, so we did our act every weekend we could get a booking.

Hugo was Cuban and came to live in the United States when Castro took over in Cuba. His wife was a trained ballerina who had done a nightclub act opening for Jimmy Durante. They met at the Tropicana nightclub in Havana when they were both working there. Hugo's act had been on the *Ed Sullivan Show*. He was handsome. Cynthia was beautiful. She was a tall, blond beauty from Sweden. She was super well-read and had a good sense of humor. They reminded me of Lucy and Desi. Matter of fact, Hugo looked

He was handsome. Cynthia was beautiful. She was a tall, blond beauty from Sweden. She was super well-read and had a good sense of humor. They reminded me of Lucy and Desi.

Ann's "weekend gig" for seven years was a nightclub act with Hugo Domenech.

like Desi and had a Cuban accent. We worked every event we could book from sportsman shows in Canada to local community affairs in Spanish Harlem.

There were many events sponsored by Cuban Americans, and they almost always ended with a dance. Hugo was a terrific dancer. So was his whole family. I loved their dancing, their food, their way of welcoming me into their family. They just adopted me. All the kids think I am Aunt Annie. I had a soul connection to the kids from the time they were born. Hugo Jr. was born with muscles. No kidding. Barbara and I sat on the swings at the local school and talked for hours. Christine, "Bunchy" to me, and I have worked together as hairstylists in the theatre.

Hugo was a terrific dancer. So was his whole family. I loved their dancing, their food, their way of welcoming me into their family. They just adopted me.

We worked our act for about seven years. Hugo had become a dolly grip. We were both working movies during the week and frequently worked the same movie. He moved the camera for cameramen, who liked him because he had natural timing. Hugo and I both became busy full time and no longer did our act. More family time for him; more social life for me. We now had our weekends to ourselves.

20.
Uncredited Stunt Work

At the time when I worked, stunt people didn't get screen credit, so I was never credited except for some of my soap opera work and maybe one feature film. Sometimes, I dated someone who asked me what kind of work I did. I said I was a movie stuntwoman. They never believed me. I guess they thought you had to be a muscle-bound hulk and live in Hollywood to do stunts in the movies. Weeks later they would say, "What do you really do? You don't look like a stuntgirl." One time a woman asked what I did, and when I said I was a stuntwoman, she asked if I was credited. I realized I was coming off like a fraud. I didn't fit the picture people had in their heads of what stuntwomen look like, and, to complicate things, I didn't get screen credit. People assume if you do a stunt, you will get credit for it. Not so much. Even now, it is the stunt coordinator who usually gets credit, if anyone does.

When I rode the diving horses, there were people who saw the act and swore it was some kind of trick. It was even suggested that the horse was a wind-up toy! Some said they were forced to jump. Some said there was a trap door and the floor opened under them and they fell. None of this was true, of course. The horses were

Sometimes, I dated someone who asked me what kind of work I did. I said I was a movie stuntwoman. They never believed me. I guess they thought you had to be a muscle-bound hulk and live in Hollywood to do stunts in the movies.

never forced. The ASPCA came around regularly and never found any reason to complain. The horses were very well cared for. They had frequent visits from the vet and were never forced, prodded, or mistreated. I would not have wanted to ride if that were true.

Now books are being written about Atlantic City and the Steel Pier. My pictures are being used all over the Internet and in books but never with a name credit. Sometimes I see my horse photo with another name on it. Nowadays some movies credit everyone, including who furnished the portable toilets. Times have changed.

I have never minded being uncredited, but I hate when someone else takes credit for my work. It does hurt a little when my own nieces and nephews think I'm exaggerating or even fibbing about things I have done. All their information comes from the Internet. That information is not always true either!

You never know how people will react to stunt performers. Some are positive and say, "Aren't you proud of what you did?" Others are skeptics or may even think you are shady in some way. Like if you say you're a model, you're really a prostitute, or if you are an actor and they never heard of you, you are a waiter professing to be an actor.

I was a product model, and in that capacity looks count for a big part of why you get hired, along with whether you are photogenic and can move and represent the product well. I always thought, however, that stunt work had more to do with skill and training than looks. One of the most common mistakes made by casting people and directors was to hire people who looked like the actor rather than the person who could do the stunt. The best make-up artists and hairstylists in the business work in film and can make you look like anyone or anything you want. Height and weight don't register unless you are huge or standing next to someone for comparison. Most times stunt people are so disguised and the stunt happens so fast and is shot in such a way that you are never recognized. Stunt people aren't meant to be recognized!

Most times stunt people are so disguised and the stunt happens so fast and is shot in such a way that you are never recognized. Stunt people aren't meant to be recognized!

The fantasy of what a stunt person looks like comes from the minds of people who don't know how to do stunts. It's not how big you are but how tight you're wound. It's also a Zen frame of mind. The rest is knowing HOW to do the stunt. I always think of the guy who blew himself up with dynamite and didn't get hurt. When he was asked why his ear was missing, he said that happened while he was still learning to do the trick. Seriously, there is a place in the center of the explosion that forms a vacuum, so if you know how to find that space and stay in it you will not be harmed.

The fantasy of what a stunt person looks like comes from the minds of people who don't know how to do stunts. It's not how big you are but how tight you're wound. It's also a Zen frame of mind. The rest is knowing HOW to do the stunt.

People always ask me, "Aren't you scared and isn't what you do dangerous?" I say no, but the real answer is—no, not scary or dangerous enough to stop me. There is danger. There is fear. The danger is in not knowing how—the fear is there to teach you.

Fear gives you a signal when you need to be aware there is danger. When you begin to learn "how," fear will guide you through the spots that are crucial to navigate correctly. Once you know how to do that, you will not be scared. It's the fight-or-flight response. Fear is your protector. Once you remove yourself from the emotional response, it becomes instinct. You don't think your way through. You think what you will do before, then you feel your way through. It's a muscle memory of things you have already learned and know how to do. The more you do it, the less fear and less danger there will be because you know how. You have learned the trick.

When you are young, you aren't so afraid. If you learn to do feats when you are young, you will not have fear to carry because you have already learned the trick, so you have the knowledge that makes you un-afraid. I think there is a certain knowing that people are born with, that is intuitive and automatic. It can be in any capacity. Math, music, anything. If you have this gift in physical prowess, you will not be so scared.

I was once on an interview show for my stunt work, and legendary producer/director/writer King Vidor was on that show. The host was more interested in finding out how much money I made

I seldom did more than one or two takes. Most times it was not necessary. They were usually happy with my first take.

than talking to King Vidor. I was flabbergasted! The host was a fairly young man. Maybe Vidor was before his time. (He should have done his homework!) Vidor's most important work was in the past at that point, but I felt honored to be on the same program with a director of his stature.

Some people find it easy to talk about how much money they make. I didn't. The host kept probing. Maybe he thought I got wealthy doing it. I didn't! Yes, there were days I made thousands, but those days were few and far between. Every stunt was not an over-the-top thriller. Fire or water could be big money. In my contract, I had on-the-set negotiating rights for those things because they weren't easy to control and could become bigger than expected. Most times I would get a double or triple union scale fee. Toward the end of my career, I had a one-take clause in my contract with additional fees for takes after the first. I didn't rehearse but would walk it for camera. I seldom did more than one or two takes. Most times it was not necessary. They were usually happy with my first take. Some people may have thought I was being difficult or arrogant. I wasn't, but by then I was doing as much or more product modeling than stunting and I couldn't afford to get beat up or spend a week recuperating. I had to work the next day.

Stunt people, like athletes, do get hurt all the time. Pulled muscles, sprains, and bruises are all common. Yes, sometimes stunt people get killed. The more times you repeat a stunt the more chance of getting hurt. It's the law of averages.

21. Soap Operas

I loved working for Joe. He was more involved than most producers and obviously loved doing what he did. He always came on the set. He had his fingers in everything and his crew was great. They always made sure the set was as I needed it to be for the stunt.

I was hired by a soap opera producer to be stunt gaffer for his show. It involved hiring stunt people, renting cars, and negotiating contracts. Yes, we did rent cars to use in stunts where they were not to be demolished. I didn't do this very long. It felt too much like office work to me, and I didn't like telling people what to do. I liked doing the stunts.

This producer, Joe Wilmore, had worked his way up from being a tour guide at NBC. In his internship somewhere along the way, he saw me do a stunt. He vowed to hire me when he got into a position to do the hiring. He did that! More than that, he introduced soaps to bigger and better stunts and began to do them on location. He even gave me the opportunity to second-direct a stunt. He would tease me by saying he had the distinction of hiring the first woman stunt coordinator. I loved working for Joe. He was more involved than most producers and obviously loved doing what he did. He always came on the set. He had his fingers in everything and his crew was great. They always made sure the set was as I needed it to be for the stunt.

Most crew guys accepted it, but a few would talk through me or around me to the stuntmen I hired. One of my guys finally told a grip. "Don't ask me. Ask her. She's my boss." All in all, it wasn't for me. I quit. I did stay on as technical adviser and did many more stunts for the show.

About this time, there was a union dispute and independent films became more popular, so there wasn't as much film done in New York. We lost a lot of our TV shows as well. Most films were now being done on location by independent companies. "Indies" is the term used for them. I did them when I got a call, but there just weren't as many calls now.

I liked print work and commercials, and I had a more predictable schedule with them, as I was paid by the hour or by the day. They didn't work into the night most times, unlike movies and TV, where once you were on the set you never knew when you would finish. It was not unusual to work from early morning until very late at night.

The still photographers were generally younger than movie people, so there were young, un-married photographers who had parties in their studios from time to time. It was part of their courting new clients and something we did as networking.

If I didn't have a stunt the next day, I could have a drink or two and not worry about it. When I was stunting, I didn't drink or party. I spent a few hours the night before a stunt visualizing. I would visualize everything that might go wrong and what I would do to compensate, then I would visualize it going perfectly. I didn't have to work out anymore—my work was a workout.

When I was stunting, I didn't drink or party. I spent a few hours the night before a stunt visualizing. I would visualize everything that might go wrong and what I would do to compensate, then I would visualize it going perfectly.

As far as visualizing went, it was one of the most effective tools in my bag of tricks, although it is not a "trick." It is a very effective way to center yourself on the stunt and make sure you are prepared for anything that might go wrong. If you have visualized every possible scenario, you will react automatically as you have visualized, because you are familiar with that scenario. I think it is a form of meditation. Some might call it "psyching yourself up." I call it centering.

When I talk about stunt work it is my way of doing things. Everyone has their own way. I can only speak for myself.

Visualizing was part of my preparation. Like an actor prepares for a role. Except with a stunt, the prep is just for your head. You have to put yourself in a psychological safe space. Once you commit to doing a stunt, you can't change your mind midstream. So you have to decide beforehand and follow through. You can't *try* to do it. You have to *do it*. When you visualize, all the "what ifs" get taken care of. The fear of the moment is dealt with when you make up your mind you will follow through.

Once you commit to doing a stunt, you can't change your mind midstream. So you have to decide beforehand and follow through.

I should say something about stair falls here because I was always doing a stair fall for one soap or another. I think I did a million of them. I only used pads in the most important places. Coccyx bone, elbows, and knees, that's about it. The trick for stairs is to relax; it will do itself. I never got hurt doing a stair fall. You just make sure you have the momentum and don't hold back. It happens so fast you can't believe it. Just keep your chin up so your face stays away from the stairs and you'll be fine.

I had to audition for it three times. She kept saying I was too pretty. I made myself uglier and used a different wig each audition; she didn't know I was the same person.

22. A New Leaf

I did a movie called *A New Leaf*. Walter Matthau starred and Elaine May wrote, directed, and co-starred in it. I was her stunt person. I had to audition for it three times. She kept saying I was too pretty. I made myself uglier and used a different wig each audition; she didn't know I was the same person. There was a scene in which Elaine May's character was to go over a waterfall in a canoe and Matthau had lines

During the filming of A New Leaf *in 1969, an assistant director shows Ann where to begin crashing a canoe and where he wants her to finish.*

Behind the towel, Matthau nips at a flask of brandy after a long day of filming.

he yelled to her from the shore. Walter kept flubbing his lines so I had to keep doing the stunt over and over. He came to me and apologized. He said that May kept rewriting the script every night so he would learn his lines and then she would change them. I said, "Don't worry. You're just putting money in my pocket," as I had a clause in my contract for extra takes, extra pay. I told him if he kept it up too long, though, they might think we were trying to scam them. He said, "Well, it's okay—they think I'm working for them, but they're really working for me." He was delightful and really funny.

I was in the water first thing every morning. October in Maine is pretty chilly, and Walter was afraid I would be chilled and get sick. He had a flask of brandy and after each day's work, he would come to me and we would have a nip. What was supposed to be two or three days of work turned into almost two months. Even though I had gone under the waterfall on a rope to check where I could find a path of least resistance, the fact that I had to repeat the stunt over and over left me with a swollen knee and a large bruise to the bone on one leg.

Since you can't control every aspect of a stunt, you more than likely will have to repeat the same injury if you do it again. There was a small opening between two huge boulders at the bottom of the falls. I could be sure from experience that I would go through that opening, but depending where the water pushed me, I would hit a rock with some force. There was no way around it. This is how you get beat up. Hazard of the profession. It comes with the territory.

There was a small opening between two huge boulders at the bottom of the falls. I could be sure from experience that I would go through that opening, but depending where the water pushed me, I would hit a rock with some force.

I never broke bones or had really serious injuries from my work, but I frequently had bruises, cuts, and pulled muscles. If you are in shape and your muscles are hard, you don't feel it much when it hap-

Veteran actor and Oscar winner Walter Matthau appeared in more than one hundred films.

Matthau checks to make sure Ann is okay following the canoe crash scene.

pens. Sprains and tendinitis take longer to heal. I once dislocated a shoulder riding the diving horse. It still bothers me once in a while. It might be something like carpel tunnel. We didn't have all the sports medicine and therapy then either. We taped each other up and kept working.

When I saw A *New Leaf*, my scene went by so fast it was like nothing. Most of what I had done went on the cutting room floor. This happens a lot.

When I saw A New Leaf, my scene went by so fast it was like nothing. Most of what I had done went on the cutting room floor. This happens a lot.

Sometimes I felt overpaid, sometimes underpaid, but it all averaged out. There really was no good way to judge before the shoot, and things usually changed by the time you got to the stunt—for better or for worse.

23.
The Exorcist

I did a backbend and walked around the room that way. Then he told me he wanted something that looked gross or unusual. I don't remember the exact words he used, but I got the idea.

In 1973, I got a call from a casting office about a film called *The Exorcist*. They needed someone to do a stunt that involved walking backwards down a flight of stairs in a backbend. I assured them it would not be a problem for me. They set up an appointment for me to meet the director, William Friedkin. I auditioned in his suite at the Sherry-Netherland Hotel. There was someone else there, I'm guessing an assistant. I did a backbend and walked around the room that way. Then he told me he wanted something that looked gross or unusual. I don't remember the exact words he used, but I got the idea. I improvised some contortions for him, we talked a few minutes, and I left.

I got the call a few days later. I was to report to the old Fox studio on 54th Street, where the interiors were being done. When I arrived to sign my contract, a rehearsal schedule was set up for me. I didn't usually rehearse, but this was not a normal stunt. It was more of an acrobatic feat. Doing a backbend is one thing. Walking down a staircase that way is something else entirely.

A safety belt and wire were already there on the stairs where I rehearsed. I did not use them. Safety belts and wires are used to

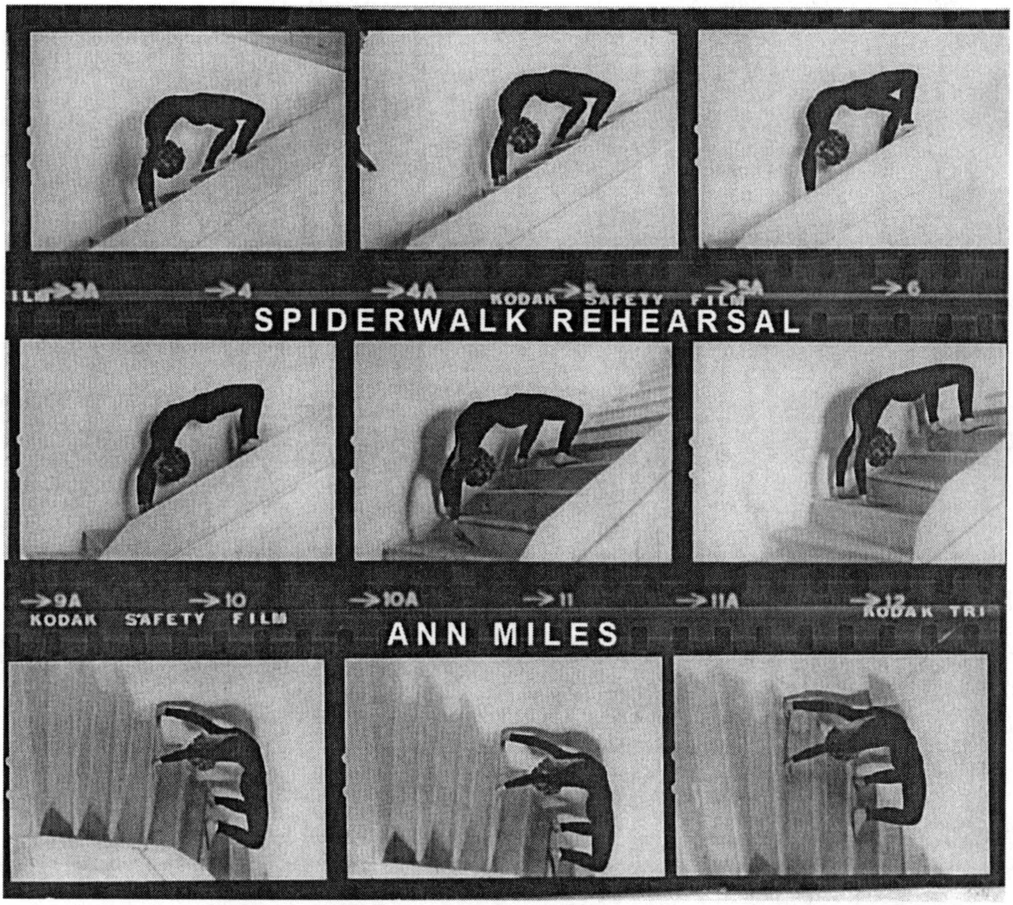

catch a fall when you are learning a new trick, but I could already do the trick. I did not need them. Rehearsal is for polish so shooting time will not be wasted. I used my rehearsal time to adjust my body line for more stability on the stairs. As a gymnast, I knew that the center of gravity on a woman is in the hips. That's where we carry most of our weight. As you go down the stairs, your hips get higher. Your head gets lower and goes under. Your head is heavy, too. The center of gravity changes and your hips want to follow the head. Where your head goes, your body wants to follow. The farther down the stairs you go, the harder it is to keep from going all the way over. I took some of the arch out of my back and put more space between my hands and feet. That way I could sort of drag my hips along in a lower position to keep from going over.

Ann scurries down the steps in a backbend as she rehearses the spiderwalk stunt for The Exorcist. *She did the stunt in rehearsals and in the actual filming without the support of wires or a harness.*

I did not rehearse on the set. There was a different staircase in a part of the studio away from the set, so I rehearsed there. This was a large studio and, for all I knew, they could have been shooting something else on the set. I was pretty much segregated from the rest of the studio.

The staircase was wider than the set and curved at the bottom. It was even easier when I got on the set. I had a fairly brief rehearsal period (one or two weeks) and one shooting day. On my shooting day, special effects insisted I wear a safety belt with piano wires. I didn't need it, I didn't want it, and it didn't work. It is expensive to insure stunt people. Sometimes, when they do not insure you for the day, they want you to take precautions they *think* will help. That's what I thought was happening. I didn't do the Spiderwalk with any help from a wire. I did it in spite of the wire. It didn't keep me from doing it. I did the Spiderwalk on my own with my full weight on the stairs just as I had rehearsed it. I did not and could not wear the harness. I was not suspended on or supported by a harness or wire. I know it seems logical that being suspended on a wire would help. It does not! It is counter-intuitive. I needed to anchor my weight on the stairs in order to control my balance. If any tension was put on the wire, it broke. They kept trying to put it back. Piano wires are not strong enough to hold a woman's weight, so it just hung there loose and unnecessary most of the time. You cannot give anyone acrobatic skills they don't have by mechanical means. Special effects are done by mechanical means. The Spiderwalk is not a special effect. It is an acrobatic stunt.

I was not suspended on or supported by a harness or wire. I know it seems logical that being suspended on a wire would help. It does not! It is counter-intuitive. I needed to anchor my weight on the stairs in order to control my balance.

So I would look like Regan (the demonically possessed girl who is the movie's main character), William Farley attached my wig and Dick Smith did my make-up on the set. There was very little make-up, and it was never retouched. Farley adjusted and secured my wig after the wire broke. The wire breaking knocked me off balance, and I fell halfway down the stairs. Thank God I wasn't using blood yet. That could have been a huge mess and would have delayed the shoot.

I landed on my feet at the bottom of the stairs and after a few seconds said I was all right. Nobody had asked. It wasn't exactly a warm and fuzzy set. I was never introduced to cinematographer Owen Roizman even though he shot my scene.

My stunt seemed to be under the umbrella of the special effects department. At the time, I didn't understand why. Nothing about this job or the whole project seemed very usual to me. I just took it in stride. William Friedkin was polite and friendly, but he never talked to me about the stunt. The only thing he talked to me about on my shooting day was the blood capsule. I was given a blood capsule, and he told me to bite it halfway down the stairs and open my mouth wide at the bottom of the stairs. That's what I did, and that little capsule the size of a One A Day vitamin poured out so much blood I thought I would choke. It had no taste, thankfully, but it immediately flooded my nose and mouth. I couldn't breathe. I could feel it coming out my nose and mouth. I had to open my mouth a little to get some air, but there was too much blood to draw in a breath so I just held my breath until I opened wide at the bottom.

William Friedkin was polite and friendly, but he never talked to me about the stunt. The only thing he talked to me about on my shooting day was the blood capsule.

This stunt was the kind of thing I was familiar with as a gymnast and, by the time I did it in 1973, I was an experienced stuntwoman and professional acrobat. It was not something I had a really hard time doing. That is not to say it was easy. It was something few stunt people would be able to do. But I specialized in this sort of feat. Unless Cirque du Soleil was in town, the chances of them finding another girl in Manhattan who could do it were slim to none.

My scene was done toward the end of the film shoot, so not long after, I got an invitation to the wrap party. It was at the wrap party that I met Barton Heyman. He was the actor who played Dr. Klein, Regan's doctor in the film. He was dressed all in black, and I thought he was a priest. There were several priests there. As soon as I talked to him, I knew he was Dr. Klein. Barton was very funny! Ellen Burstyn and Linda Blair were there, too.

When I left the party, Barton hailed a cab and offered to drop me off. He did and got my phone number. He took me to the New York premiere of *The Exorcist*. It was a hoot! People screamed and jumped and hid their eyes. It was electric. Of course, I looked for my scene, but it wasn't there. I put "*Exorcist* Spiderwalk" on my stunt résumé all the same. I had done the stunt.

Of course, I looked for my scene, but it wasn't there. I put "Exorcist Spiderwalk" on my stunt résumé all the same. I had done the stunt.

Barton and I became good friends, and we worked together a few times after *The Exorcist*. We dated for a while and stayed friends until his death in 1996.

24.
Surprise

What happened next came out of left field. People lined up around the block to see *The Exorcist* in bitter-cold winter weather. Some countries banned it, such as England. Reviews were from one extreme to the other. It caused a huge commotion all over the world. It was one of the highest-grossing films of all time and became a cultural phenomenon. It won awards and acclaim. There would be sequels and horror movie spoofs. People talked about every detail of the film, including the scenes that were excluded from the original film. Sometime in the next thirty years, the Spiderwalk scene became the most famous missing scene of the film. It was legendary and iconic, and it had not yet been seen. Myths grew up about how it was done, who did it, and why it was excluded from the original film. This information came from news interviews, magazine articles, and the like done by Marcel Vercoutere, who was in charge of special effects. As soon as the Internet was available, Vercoutere had a website that put out even more false information, including giving Linda R. Hager credit for the Spiderwalk. That website was in full force through 2013 when Vercoutere died due to complications with dementia.

Sometime in the next thirty years, the Spiderwalk scene became the most famous missing scene of the film. It was legendary and iconic, and it had not yet been seen.

There was nothing I could do. How can you challenge something nobody has ever seen? I thought the scene would never be released, so I let it go.

Vercoutere said he built a carriage and flying wires. He said he put Hager in his harness because she couldn't *turn over*. He said he connected her to his carriage above so he could lift her just high enough to touch the stairs with her hands and feet—not possible. This did NOT happen.

I knew this could not be true. He was speaking about the harness made to jerk actress Linda Blair on the bed. The harness he was talking about was made of metal with a hard plaster-like covering. It went halfway up her back, and over that was a leather corset that laced up the sides and then had leather straps that buckled in the front. Hager, wearing that harness, would not have had the flexibility to arch her back at all and could not have come anywhere near the stairs with her hands and feet. Her spine would have been disengaged. As he said, she would only be able to move her arms and legs. He said he would release her at just the right moment and she would turn over and finish the shot the right way up. Never mind he had already said she could not *turn over* and there was no automatic release on his rig. Someone would have had to physically go to her and unhook the wires. "Just the right moment" would have come and gone. Even if she had been able to turn over and stand up, she was still in the harness. Trying to finish the shot that way would have been Frankenstein-ish.

But what difference did it make? There was nothing I could do. How can you challenge something nobody has ever seen? I thought the scene would never be released, so I let it go. I assumed it would be hot for a little while then be gone. Boy, was I wrong about that! Anyway, I had to think about how to make a living now that my stunt career was taking a nose dive.

The Spiderwalk just kept getting more attention over the years. Thirty years passed before the production company decided to release *The Exorcist (The Version You've Never Seen)* in 2000. The Spiderwalk scene was included, but by that time Marcel's fabrication was entrenched on the Internet and ingrained in the public's mind. Linda R. Hager got credit for my work. To this day, I have not been able to get her name removed from my work. Some websites get it that she did not do the Spiderwalk scene, some seem to think her false publicity applies to me, and some say that we both did it.

To this day, I have not been able to get her name removed from my work.

I decided it might be time for a career change that didn't depend on youth, beauty, or physical prowess. After all, I was approaching 40 years of age. I decided on theatrical hairstyling.

25. Hairstyling and Barbering

I continued to do stunt work and modeling through the 1970s, but over those years my workload started to dwindle. I had "*Exorcist* Spiderwalk" listed as a credit on my stunt résumé. It should have been a wonderful credit for me. I was not aware at the time, however, of the reams of Spiderwalk publicity and Internet coverage that credited it to someone else. My credibility and my stunt career were damaged. Agents who saw this no longer trusted me. I was accused of padding my résumé. Lots of artists did this, but I did not. I know that if you didn't witness what happened in those years, it is hard to imagine. People went crazy!

As I had more days off now, I decided it might be time for a career change that didn't depend on youth, beauty, or physical prowess. After all, I was approaching 40 years of age. I decided on theatrical hairstyling. I had always been interested in it, and I could still be on the set—not on camera anymore but behind the camera.

I had to get a cosmetology license and serve a three-year apprenticeship with the make-up and hairstylist union. After I graduated from Wilfred Academy, I went to barber school. Then I worked in an old-fashioned barbershop in the furrier district of Manhattan. I was an apprentice to four barbers. They were all Italian and all experts in everything, from old-style clipper cuts to the then-popular longer styles for men. They still did straight-razor shaving and barber massages (scalp and facial). I wanted to learn it all. Paul, the owner, hired me and agreed to let me apprentice because he wanted to offer perms in the shop and I could do perms since I had a cosmetology license.

There was a boot black, a manicurist, myself, and four Italian barbers. Oh my god—it was a riot! Lady barbers were still pretty much non-existent at the time. Perms for men and unisex shops were just starting to appear. I wanted to learn men's styling and cuts for movie work.

Because I was an apprentice, I only got paid one hundred dollars a week. I worked eight hours a day six days a week. Saturdays were slow. Only two barbers and I came in, so they let me practice cutting their hair and shaving them.

I had negotiated with Paul for time off when I got a stunt job or a modeling job, which wasn't so often anymore. Obviously, I couldn't live in Manhattan on one hundred dollars a week. There was a TV in the shop, and they got a kick out of seeing me fall down the stairs on a soap opera. Paul was a great mentor, laid-back and easygoing. He liked for me to look nice in a skirt during the week. I could wear jeans on Saturday. Most of our customers were furriers, but there were other businessmen from the neighborhood and walk-ins of every description. Later, when I was allowed to work, I got the walk-ins.

Paul had organized a workshop for shop owners. They would meet every week or two at one of the owners' shops and have a guest expert. These experts were champion men stylists or shop owners who specialized in razor cuts or singeing or longer styles for men or, my favorite, precision cuts. Paul allowed me to participate in these workshops. I had to bring a model to work on. The experts,

I was an apprentice to four barbers. They were all Italian and all experts in everything, from old-style clipper cuts to the then-popular longer styles for men.

mostly Italian, were adept at hands-on teaching. They went around the shop helping and showing each person. They demanded perfection. They were in-your-face, cutting-edge professionals. (No pun intended.) This was the best education in hair cutting and styling I could have gotten anywhere.

They demanded perfection. They were in-your-face. cutting-edge professionals. (No pun intended.) This was the best education in hair cutting and styling I could have gotten anywhere.

Meanwhile, back at the shop, I was cutting all the walk-ins. Part of the shop's service, as a courtesy with a haircut, was a trim for the customer's eyebrows, ear hair, and nose hair. If they had a mustache, you trimmed that as well. Of course, I had learned all that and I did it. Some of the walk-ins were unkempt, and a few even looked homeless or alcoholic—but they were treated just as any regular customer was treated.

This personal contact could be a difficult process for me. Too intimate. Once in a while, a customer would obviously be hitting on me. In addition, there were the barbers picking up on all of this. You could cut the vibes sometimes with a straight razor; the testosterone level was over the top. When the customer left or there was a discreet moment, one of the barbers would pinch my rear or make some comment. It wasn't sexual harassment from the barbers but good-natured teasing about the attention I got from a few customers.

It took all the coping skills I could muster to get through the initial phase of my hair styling and cutting. I did tacit self-talk through a whole haircut sometimes. I exposed myself to it until I got over it. I pinched the barbers back. I made it clear that my reason for being there was not for their entertainment. As in the beginning of any new endeavor, it was a rough spot I had to get past.

One day, a dirty, unfortunate walk-in with thick, overgrown hair came in. Oh, and he had a bad cold, complete with runny nose. It was my last customer of the day, and I was going to make the best of it. I gave him a nice consultation: How short did he want to go? Would he like his hair thinned, above the ears traditional, or over the ears modern? Blow dry or natural? I took my time with his shampoo, and I was going to pay for it if need be. I thinned his hair and gave him a great precision cut. Then, I got a Kleenex and ask him to blow his nose. I took a hot towel from the warmer and placed it on his face. I pressed it in for a few seconds then wiped his face and nose as I took it off. I then trimmed his eyebrows, his ear hair, and his nose hair. He was so polite and grateful it almost made me cry. He paid his bill and left. I was finished for the day.

I went upstairs to my locker, and I did cry. One of the barbers came up, saw me crying, and asked what was wrong. I said I didn't think I could go on doing this and I wanted to quit. Another barber came up. They both told me that they felt the same in the beginning and I was only going to be there for a year. When I got into theatrical hairstyling, I would never have to do that kind of work again. They were right! I stayed.

When my year was up, I left. The whole experience is one of my fondest memories. I was certainly much better for having done it. I was a competent haircutter and stylist for men as well as women now. I went to the local union to seek apprenticeship. It was a three-year commitment, but you got paid if you were called to work. You could only work if all the union members were called first. Of course, you got all the jobs members didn't want and they could call you anytime, day or night, to be somewhere in half an hour. I did news, game shows, soap operas, *Saturday Night Live*, etc. I even cut the male extras' hair for the movie *Raging Bull*.

When my year was up, I left. The whole experience is one of my fondest memories. I was certainly much better for having done it.

Bob was a wonderful character. He looked like a longshoreman or a sailor. He was very friendly and outgoing with a big heart. He was always open to helping you out if he could.

26. Bob Kelly Wig Creations

Since I wasn't working full time, I decided to further my education by going to Bob Kelly Wig Creations to apprentice in wig making and styling. Wigs, bald pates, and facial hair pieces are all used extensively in movies, television, and theatre.

Bob Kelly was the make-up artist on the first commercial I ever did. He was very nice to me, and he had put in a good word for me at the union when I wanted to become a hairstylist. Bob owned the premier wig factory in New York City. Bob was a wonderful character. He looked like a longshoreman or a sailor. He was very friendly and outgoing with a big heart. He was always open to helping you out if he could. The first time I met him he was wearing jeans and a mink jacket. Custom made, of course.

Bob made and supplied wigs for movies, TV, soaps, commercials, and theatre. He had a line of Bob Kelly theatrical make-up as well. I was always being sent to him for a wig fitting for something I was doing. I was there so much we had become friends over the years. If I needed a wig for pictures or an audition he would loan me one he pulled out of a drawer. (He had drawers full of wigs.) When he did wigs for Broadway shows and movies, they were all custom made for each actor. I was fitted for custom-made, human-hair wigs for a few commercials. These were not cheap, commercial synthetics. These were top-of-the-line, made-to-order, human-hair wigs.

I was an apprentice at the factory for about a year, where I learned everything about wigs and prosthetic facial hair. I learned how to nail wigs to wooden blocks to shampoo, dye, or perm them. Styling, too, of course. They were pinned to canvas blocks for styling. I learned how to measure and fit wigs. Also, how to ventilate (hooking hair into a net with a metal hook similar to a crochet hook). I learned how to attach facial hair and how to clean and care for it. Also, I learned how to groom facial hair with tiny curling irons.

In short, I learned everything about wigs and facial hair. It stood me in good stead. I came in whenever I wanted, and I could go on a union call if I got one. Bob supplied all the wigs for *Saturday Night Live*. Linda Rice, the person in charge of styling and delivering wigs to *SNL*, had a desk at Bob's. She hired me to do styling so I was there quite a lot. Bob and I went to lunch together over the years. After his wife died, we went out to dinner a couple of times, but we were just friends. We had a great friendship and that's how it stayed. A few years later he remarried.

I was an apprentice at the factory for about a year, where I learned everything about wigs and prosthetic facial hair. I learned how to nail wigs to wooden blocks to shampoo, dye, or perm them. Styling, too, of course.

I cut Mick's hair and told someone who asked me what I did that day, "He's some kind of rock star, I think." My friend said, no, he's THE rock star!

27. Movie Hairstylist

I started getting more work with the union, and I met Richard, a make-up apprentice who, like me, wanted to do movies. We were both still doing the union jobs we could get—but not movies. Richard had a friend who was a producer, and he produced some non-union movies. We worked those, and a German TV series that was shot in New York City. Richard did the make-up; I did the hair. These were hungry years for both of us. We did a movie called *Union City* that starred Mick Jagger and Debbie Harry (Blondie, "Heart of Glass"). I cut Mick's hair and told someone who asked me what I had done that day, "He's some kind of rock star, I think." My friend said, no, he's THE rock star!

Eventually, Richard and I both started getting more union work, but for me it was a problem. Most of the make-up and hair people knew me as a stunt performer. Most of them were wonderful to me, but there was a clique of old-biddy bitches that made my life hell. They resented my being in "their" territory and referred to me as "the stuntgirl" in the most derogatory tone they could muster.

By this time I had done enough work in TV and even movies to realize I didn't like it as much as I thought I would.

As a hairdresser, there was too much time just watching and long hours without enough to keep me from getting bored. The fact that these women worked all the time and I was constantly exposed to this abuse made it not seem worth trying to hang in when I wasn't so sure I really liked working in movies as a hairdresser. I would try theater.

As a hairdresser, there was too much time just watching and long hours without enough to keep me from getting bored.

As soon as I got my first Broadway show, I knew that was the place for me. I was home. Nobody knew me there, and I discovered I liked the work much better than hairstyling in movies or TV.

28. Broadway

Broadway was non-union at the time. As soon as I got my first Broadway show, I knew that was the place for me. I was home. Nobody knew me there, and I discovered I liked the work much better than hairstyling in movies or TV. In theatre, you work hard and are busy from the time you arrive until you leave. I love theatre people and you are more involved in the show, too. You have to do quick changes in the wings and you have "cues" throughout the show. You are in the theater every day and every night, so you make friends and get to know the people you work with. There are parties and extra activities. I got to cut hair for the show and for my own customers. The old biddies did me a huge favor!

My time spent with Bob Kelly paid off. In the theatre everyone wears a wig. It was seldom that actors were not wearing a wig, except for men. My knowledge of wigs and my knowledge of men's styling put me right up there with the best stylists on Broadway. I found theatre stylists to be even more competent than a lot of union stylists. I learned more working next to them.

People may think when you work in the theatre as a hairstylist, you just go in for a couple of hours and style wigs, put them on, take them off, then go home after the show. That doesn't even BEGIN to describe it!

Yes, there are some small shows with few actors, but more common are large shows with many actors and large dance numbers throughout the show. A drama with only a few actors may only have one stylist. Then there are musicals with up to seven stylists and more than a hundred wigs. Most of these wigs are human hair and must be taken care of as you would take care of human hair. At the beginning of a show they are delivered to the theater or rehearsal hall by the designer. They are straight from the factory, ungroomed and about a foot long. During the set-up rehearsal phase, your supervisor will assign the characters each stylist will work on. All the wigs have to be washed, cut, and styled according to the sketch or verbal instructions given to you by the designer. Sometimes, they are dyed or permed.

Actors are learning the show at this point. They rehearse without wigs, but you must learn the show along with them and figure out where and how a wig change can be done.

At this point, the space is usually limited and not yet organized. You find a space where you can. Hopefully, near an outlet for your curling irons, blow dryer, etc. You need to place your vice for holding wig blocks on a secure surface in front of a mirror if one is available.

Actors are learning the show at this point. They rehearse without wigs, but you must learn the show along with them and figure out where and how a wig change can be done. At the same time, there are hundreds of wigs that still have to be washed, conditioned, cut, and styled. They are secured to blocks and labeled with the actor's name and character name. At some point in this rehearsal process, the designer will want to see the wig on the actor and make changes as he or she sees fit. You must prep the actor's hair and put a stocking cap on him or her before securing the wig. For men with short or maybe no hair, it could be only a headband probably glued on with spirit gum. If they are to wear facial hair, that is also glued on with spirit gum or, for smaller pieces, maybe double faced tape. In some cases, beards can be attached to wigs with hairpins on each side of the cheeks. You have to be aware if

Hairstylists and actors alike have not done these changes enough to be adept, so the wigs are handled roughly. All in all, it's wig HELL! When they come off at the end of the show, they look like they have been through the mill.

the wig with facial hair has to come off and another placed on in a quick change and plan your prep accordingly.

Once the blocking of the show is set you will figure out where the actor exits and enters for wig changes, touch-ups, etc. If the actors have time, they come to the wig room for changes. If not, you will go to them, wherever they are in the wings. There are times you will go on stage (behind a set) to do changes.

By the time you get to dress rehearsal, you will have learned the show, and cut and styled twenty-plus wigs and whatever facial hair your characters use. You also will have cut some of the actors' hair if they do not wear a wig. That is also dictated by the designer. The designer must approve the look of everything you do.

After dress rehearsal, you will know your wig changes and will have chosen a music cue that allows you to get there (to the changing place) or be prepared for the actor to come to you. Time between cues is used to work on the wigs that are not in use at the time.

Next are previews. This is the performance time between set-up and opening night. This is the time all the kinks should be worked out. This is live performance for an audience and a time when everyone is still a little nervous. The wigs go through a hard time now. Actors are sweating more than usual. Hairstylists and actors alike have not done these changes enough to be adept, so the wigs are handled roughly. All in all, it's wig HELL! When they come off at the end of the show, they look like they have been through the mill. Yes, wig hell. Some are damp and wilted or soaking wet around the edges and even smelly. Everything anti-wig has come to pass.

These wigs for the most part are delicate, with fragile lace fronts that can be easily stretched or torn and can't be man-handled without dire consequences. They are NOT cheap either. Thankfully, previews don't last long, and people and wigs calm down.

Opening Night! Openings are exciting in so many ways. If your show has generated excitement around town and the critics are nice to you, telegrams and flowers flood in from everywhere.

It is a tradition in the theatre to give opening-night gifts. You get gifts and you give gifts to everyone. Cast and crew. People come in early to leave gifts on your station or in your dressing room. The whole place is piled high with the most elaborately wrapped gifts or a bottle of champagne or both. Producers also bring opening-night gifts. You will be opening gifts all through the show when you have a minute or two free.

After the show, when your wigs are blocked, you change into the new outfit you bought for the opening-night party. These parties are plush because they are meant to impress critics, producers, investors, etc. The food is fabulous and plentiful, and so is the booze. Theatre people will have a party at the drop of a hat!

You can't drink too much because early the next day, all the wigs have to be washed, set, and styled. The wigs are put in a dryer called a wig oven, so they will be dry and styled before show time. Now you can settle in and figure out your work schedule before and after each show. Wigs get washed every two weeks or so. Facial hair has to be cleaned each night and groomed each day before the show. All wigs are touched up or combed out either after the show at night or before the show each day. Depending on the period the show takes place in, some of these sets and comb-outs can be quite elaborate and time consuming.

All wigs are touched up or combed out either after the show at night or before the show each day. Depending on the period the show takes place in, some of these sets and comb-outs can be quite elaborate and time consuming.

Theatrical hairstylists I knew, myself included, hardly ever took time off; they weren't sick much, but once in a while they had to be out, so a " swing" had to be trained to come in and work just in case. These were usually stylists between shows or people who didn't want to work full time. I did it between shows in the beginning. After a while, I just went from show to show. You got hired by a supervisor, usually with the approval of the designer if it was a new show opening. If you were hired as a replacement, it was the supervisor's call. Occasionally, a designer would call you if he knew you from another show. Usually he would just mention you to the supervisor he hired.

I am still friends with Ali, my favorite swing. I made many good friends in the theatre. Even though it is hard work, has a high stress level, and demands a grueling schedule, it is also a lot of FUN! I did many hit shows and am still in touch with some wonderful people after all these years.

I made many good friends in the theatre. Even though it is hard work, has a high stress level, and demands a grueling schedule, it is also a lot of FUN!

My first show was *Beatlemania*. I got to do all those Beatle haircuts. I was the only person in the hair department. There were only a few wigs.

I went on to meet a young up-and-coming hairstylist who I worked closely with in the beginning. He was rather ambitious and a really great stylist and a great administrator. Leon and I worked on *Nicholas Nickleby*, the eight-hour version done by the Royal Shakespeare Company. We did many other shows together, such as *Barnum* where I met Terence Mann, my favorite Broadway actor. We went on later to do *Cats*.

29.
Cats and More

When I came in for work early that night, I could hardly get the door open because there were flowers all over the place. They were all over the floor and lining the stairs all the way up three flights to the hair room. Oh, it was glorious!

Cats was the first big blockbuster show and would change Broadway forever. Terence Mann played Rum Tum Tugger, the rock star cat. The *Cats* opening night was unforgettable! When I came in for work early that night, I could hardly get the door open because there were flowers all over the place. They were all over the floor and lining the stairs all the way up three flights to the hair room. Oh, it was glorious! Opening-night gifts were piled high. It was already a smash hit. Telegrams poured in from around the world.

Leon and I set up that show and worked it for quite a while. The wigs were dyed in crazy colors with spots like cats have. Paul Huntley was the designer. We touched some of them up between dye jobs with markers. Make-up was heavy duty, and most of the wigs were glued on with spirit gum.

The show just ran forever, and I stayed for a long time. I can't remember how long, but Leon said I was into menopause and had become a bitch. He was probably right. We had some disagreement and went our separate ways. Now Broadway was taken into the union and I got my union card.

I remembered how happy I was working *Cats*. Working that show was like a never-ending animal house. Well yeah. *Cats*... It was a riot!

I went on to some wonderful shows, all top hits. I did Disney's first Broadway show, *Beauty and the Beast*. Terry Mann was the original Beast, and I was his personal hairstylist. Not only did he have hair on his head, but he had hair all over. He had a tail and lots of facial hair. He had lots of wigs for the Beast and Prince characters. His Beast wigs were huge. Prince wigs were long. They were fabulous! Bob Kelly made them. I permed, cut, and styled all of it including the tail and chest piece, and I cut his own hair, too. He was my star and the only actor I worked on. That was enough to keep me more than busy. David Lawrence was the hair designer. Linda Rice was the hair supervisor.

We previewed in Austin, Texas, and the sets were huge. Since it was Disney's first Broadway musical, things were really rough. They flew huge sets over your head as you moved backstage to your cues. It was very scary in the beginning. Once we got to Broadway, it finally smoothed out. I just loved working with Terry. He was a wonderful Beast and a great personality—in-your-face, upbeat, and fun.

After Terry left, it wasn't the same for me. My dad got cancer, and I went home to take care of him. Mother had died the year before. Daddy died seven months after I got home. He had gone into banking in his mid-forties and had done well at it. I settled his estate, then returned to Manhattan. Barton Heyman, who I met on *The Exorcist* and had stayed friends with, died two days after I came back. I saw him for dinner the night before he died. He had gone to the opening-night party of *Beauty and the Beast* with me. It seemed everyone around me was going out of my life.

I remembered how happy I was working *Cats*. Working that show was like a never-ending animal house. Well yeah, *Cats*... It was a riot! The girl dancers were wild and came in all sizes and shapes. The English designer fell in love with one of them even before we opened and they would be glued together in the hallway as you passed going to your cue. The dance choreographer, way past menopause, had a young boyfriend who came to visit. She was a cougar before it was in vogue.

I was waiting in a little change room next to the stage one night and Cary Grant came in looking for Dyan Cannon. Other nights Michael Jackson or Al Pacino came backstage and mingled with the cast and crew. There was never a dull moment.

I was waiting in a little change room next to the stage one night and Cary Grant came in looking for Dyan Cannon. Other nights Michael Jackson or Al Pacino came backstage and mingled with the cast and crew. There was never a dull moment.

One of the lighting guys had a hot fling with someone in the show. It was not discreet, and she gave a running account in the dressing room every night. T.M.I. Nothing was left to the imagination. Terry as Tugger was so sexy that conservative theatergoers were shocked and appalled. They called it dirty sex. Yeah,Terry! ROCK 'N' ROLL!

One of the gay wardrobe girls had a crush on me. Everywhere I turned, she was there. Leon teased me like crazy. That's the first and last time that ever happened to me (as far as I know).

I had so much fun working that show! When I left, the girls gave me a going-away party. When we left the theater, we walked right into a drug bust behind the Winter Garden Theatre. One of the girls got hauled off to jail for not moving down the street when told to. She was held for two or three hours. We all met up later at a tavern in the Hell's Kitchen area. Oh my, what a blast!

We did a commercial for New York with Frank Sinatra while I was at *Cats*. There was so much extra stuff that I was exhausted when I left. I tried to retire, but I couldn't afford to so I came back to work and went on to do many more shows.

Now I was working mostly for David Brown, my favorite Broadway hair designer. In 2017, David Brown won the Drama Desk Award for Outstanding Wig and Hair Design for the Broadway show *War Paint*. He had a crew of stylists he tended to use more often than not. I got to work with Richard Orton, who I had worked with before, and I met Larry Boyette. We three worked together on several shows: *Steel Pier*, *Sideshow*, and *Annie Get Your Gun*. Sonia Rivera was with us on *Steel Pier*. Sonia did the most

President George H. W. Bush and First Lady Barbara Bush stopped by the hair room to chat with us one night. They seemed like they belonged there. It was sweet.

exquisite finger waves I have ever seen and she made it look easy! And she couldn't stay on our diet any better than I could, but at least we tried.

Bernadette Peters was Annie. She was one of the sweetest, most down-to-earth actors I ever worked with. We all stayed on and did it with Reba McEntire, who made the show a hit all over again. She was friendly and nice to everyone.

President George H. W. Bush and First Lady Barbara Bush stopped by the hair room to chat with us one night. They seemed like they belonged there. It was sweet. They were sweet.

30. Spiderwalk

The truth is that in 1973 special effects supervisor Marcel Vercoutere presented the Spiderwalk to the press *as if* it were one of his special effects. The press picked this up and ran with it.

Fans want to know…

What is the truth about the Spiderwalk? Why did it take so long to get out? How difficult was it to do? People still ask and want to know.

The truth is that in 1973 special effects supervisor Marcel Vercoutere presented the Spiderwalk to the press *as if* it were one of his special effects. The press picked this up and ran with it. Marcel was publicized as the special effects wizard who made the Spiderwalk possible, and he gave Linda R. Hager credit for my work. But Marcel's account was not accurate. *It just did not happen!* Only principal actors were filmed for the scene he spoke of (scene 143 non-bloody). His harness and wire rig were never used in the Spiderwalk at all. *Linda R. Hager never performed the Spiderwalk or even attempted it. This publicity is bogus and does not apply to me.* There is NO film of Hager and there are NO images of her. *All film and all images of the Spiderwalk are Ann Miles.* Hager was a stand-in (lighting double) erroneously credited for my work.

When I read Marcel's account of filming the Spiderwalk scene (scene 143) I knew his account was not true and would be impossible to do. But my scene (scene 143A) was not included in the original film. It was not released for thirty years, so Marcel's story could not be challenged. During those three decades, the Spiderwalk became iconic and legendary. I would have to see the film before I could say it was my footage. I saw it. It was mine.

Meanwhile, Marcel was still doing interviews. In 1983, he did an interview for *Fangoria* magazine in which he talked about another Spiderwalk scene in which "the girl" runs across the floor and bites someone on the leg. *This never happened either.*

Despite the fact that the Spiderwalk had not been seen, it became a sensation. People loved talking about it. It has action figures, photos, and T-shirts. Now there is a Spiderwalk doll. Although missing, the Spiderwalk scene was one of the most-talked-about scenes in the film.

Despite the fact that the Spiderwalk had not been seen, it became a sensation. People loved talking about it.

This photo is from the actual filming of Ann Miles performing the spiderwalk stunt and was used in The Exorcist (The Version You've Never Seen), *released in 2000.*

In 1997, the BBC did a documentary, *Fear of God*. Marcel Vercoutere participated in that documentary. William Friedkin did an interview with Mark Kermode prior to the making of the documentary, and Friedkin said he did not remember shooting a Spiderwalk scene. While working on the documentary, Kermode found my film and pulled it out of the Warner Bros. archive where it had been for thirty years. It was not labeled with my name. They used part of my film to splice onto Linda Blair in the non-bloody stair crawl for the documentary. Then Friedkin put together the Bloody Spiderwalk for 2000's *The Exorcist (The Version You've Never Seen)*. I must say he did a great job of it, too. It was chilling!

I came forward to my union, SAG-AFTRA. They checked with Warner Bros., who said they were not using my film. They were of course using my work, but they did not know it. This back-and-forth went on for a few more years. I finally located John McGuire and Leif Larson at SAG-AFTRA. John told me that I would have to prove what I was telling him. He wasn't encouraging. He said it was stale and that thirty years later people who worked on my scene would not remember or would be dead or retired. All the same, I did prove that I alone performed the Spiderwalk. When confronted by SAG-AFTRA, Hager signed a notarized statement saying she did not perform the stunt. Leif Larson was responsible for getting that done.

I finally located John McGuire and Leif Larson at SAG-AFTRA. John told me that I would have to prove what I was telling him. He wasn't encouraging.

By the time *The Exorcist (The Version You've Never Seen)* was released in 2000, Vercoutere's and Hager's names were ingrained in people's minds all over the world. The Spiderwalk myth stuck like glue. All the books that were now being written took their research from false information. Mark Kermode wrote his book, and since Friedkin did not remember shooting Spiderwalk footage, Vercoutere was more than happy to fill in the gaps. Unfortunately for me, all the pages about the Spiderwalk in Kermode's book are full of incorrect information. Vercoutere *confirmed* to Kermode that film was shot of Hager and it got "kinda bloody." He convinced all of them that the film Kermode found was Hager and that it was sc. 143, the non-bloody scene, and it had gotten bloody. *This never happened.* It was at this time that Marcel started all the prattle about removing wires with computer-generated imagery (CGI). Now there was a new reason for them to continue to talk about his wire. It is my understanding that they "cleaned up" the whole film with CGI and retouched a couple of frames. The Spiderwalk film was sped up, but that was the only alteration. I don't think anyone saw any wires until they put it on the Internet so it could be slowed it down and people could stop it at will. Now CGI has become the big topic of conversation.

Now the myth got even bigger, with media spin, rumors of more Spiderwalk scenes, CGI blood, CGI removal of wires, use of harness and wire rig, things people heard or read, and things people just made up or took for granted.

Chatting about how someone did something they did not do is like adults playing the Telephone Game on the Internet, don't you think?

Chatting about how someone did something they did not do is like adults playing the Telephone Game on the Internet. don't you think?

31. SAG-AFTRA

What could I do? SAG-AFTRA said I had to prove my claim to them. I eventually got help from John McGuire, senior negotiator at SAG-AFTRA. Considering his position there, he was not obligated to help me. But he did, and I am extremely grateful because without his help this would never have gotten any consideration. He got Warner Bros. to pull Marcel's website in 2013. I was told it was on a pirated website. Leif Larson at SAG-AFTRA was instrumental in finally securing a notarized statement from Linda R. Hager saying she did not perform the Spiderwalk. Now, I have proof!

I am still having trouble correcting my records and getting Hager's name off my work. Search engines and websites take information only from reliable published sources. I got reliable published sources and have submitted them—only to be ignored. And erroneous information in circulation on the Internet keeps me from being fairly vetted for my current writing projects.

I eventually got help from John McGuire, senior negotiator at SAG-AFTRA. Considering his position there, he was not obligated to help me. But he did, and I am extremely grateful because without his help this would never have gotten any consideration.

WARNER BROS.
PICTURES

VIA U.S. & ELECTRONIC MAIL

October 15, 2014

John McGuire
SAG-AFTRA
1900 Broadway
5th Floor
New York, NY 10023

RE: "Exorcist" and Ann Miles

Dear John:

Thank you for sending me the statement signed by Linda Hager confirming that she, in fact, did not perform the "spider walk" scene for the theatrical motion picture "Exorcist". Based upon this written acknowledgement and other information you shared with me, Warner Bros. Pictures is able to credit Ms. Ann Miles as the performer who performed the "spider walk" scene on promotional material. Of course, there is no contractual requirement in the SAG Basic Agreement to accord credit to performers on promotional material. Ms. Miles also did not negotiate better terms and conditions with respect to credit in her personal services agreement. Furthermore, as I've mentioned before, Warner Bros. Pictures has never credited any performer (whether it be Linda Hager or any other performer) with the spider walk scene in the DVD, Blu-Ray or promotional material. Simply stated, there is nothing to correct. Notwithstanding the foregoing, due to Warner Bros. Pictures Labor Relations' longstanding relationship with you and out of courtesy to Ms. Miles, we are willing to accord her credit for performing this scene on promotional material on a non-citable, non-precedential basis.

Unfortunately, we cannot accord her special screen credit on newly distributed Blu-Rays and DVD's. We have fulfilled our screen credit obligations under the SAG Agreement for the theatrical release and subsequent releases of the "Exorcist" into supplemental markets. You relayed to me Ms. Miles' request to correct the spelling of her name as it appears in the cast credits on the website IMDB.com. As we discussed earlier, Warner Bros. Pictures does not submit screen credits for its theatrical motion pictures to this website. I would suggest that Ms. Miles contact IMDB directly.

If you should have any questions, please do not hesitate to contact me.

Best,

Jane Lee

Jane C. Lee
Senior Labor Relations Counsel

A Division of WB Studio Enterprises Inc.
A Warner Bros. Entertainment Company

4000 Warner Boulevard, Burbank, California 91522

SAG·AFTRA.

To Whom It May Concern:

I, Linda Rae Hagar, hereby affirm and acknowledge that I did not perform the stunt commonly known as the "Bloody Spider Walk" during the filming of the original "The Exorcist." Although I worked on that film, I did not have the physical skill or training to perform such an acrobatic movement as walking upside down on my hands and feet backwards down the stairs with my back arched.
Please take this as such proof as necessary to see that the appropriate person is given the credit for that performance.
Sincerely,

(Print Name) LINDA R. Hager

(Sign Name) Linda R Hagar

Date signed 7/13/15

STEPHANIE A. PERRY
NOTARY PUBLIC, STATE OF NEW YORK
Registration No. 02PE6130447
Qualified in New York County
Commission Expires November 19, 2017

Stephanie Ann Perry
July 13, 2015

SCREEN ACTORS GUILD-AMERICAN FEDERATION of TELEVISION and RADIO ARTISTS
Associated Actors & Artistes of America / AFL-CIO

SAGAFTRA.org
855.SAG·AFTRA / 855.724.2387

TO WHOM IT MAY CONCERN,

I ANN MILES, ATTEST THAT ALL THE FOOTAGE OF THE EXORCIST SPIDERWALK EVER SEEN AND NOW BEING SHOWN IS MY FOOTAGE.

I ANN MILES, AM THE CONTORTIONIST STUNT PERSON HIRED SOLELY TO DO THE SPIDERWALK AND I AM THE <u>ONLY</u> PERSON WHO DID THE SPIDERWALK.

ALL SPIDERWALK STILL PICTURES SOLD ON EBAY ARE MYSELF.

Ann Miles

Ann Miles

6-18-2014

Jackie Kendrick

6-18-2014

JACKIE KENDRICK
NOTARY PUBLIC
GRANT CO., ARKANSAS

32.

It's a Wrap

My request for a screen credit on DVDs and Blu-ray was denied. I did not negotiate for better terms and conditions in my original contract. Of course, in 1973 there was no DVD or Blu-ray. There was no Internet either.

My request for a screen credit on DVDs and Blu-ray was denied. I did not negotiate for better terms and conditions in my original contract. Of course, in 1973 there was no DVD or Blu-ray. There was no Internet either. Warner Bros.' word would have meant the Internet would correct itself.

I can't say I'm surprised. I am disappointed! This means all the untrue publicity will stand, as is, and the film has gone into the Warner Bros. and Smithsonian archives with Hager's name on the Spiderwalk. Even with verification that I am the only person who did the Spiderwalk, submitted to websites and book publishers, very little has changed. My correction attempts concerning the truth about the Spiderwalk have been primarily ignored. However, Daniel Eagan's publication *America's Film Legacy 2009-2010* published by Bloomsbury has been corrected to give credit as the Spiderwalk performed by Ann Miles.

Every old, worn-out saying you've ever heard pops into my head. Like: You can't put the genie back in the bottle. Chicken one day and feathers the next. Everything happens for a reason. Honesty is the best policy, and on and on.

Publicity and press do have a way of sometimes getting carried away. That's showbiz. All in all, people had fun with it and still do! So what the hell.

I had a boyfriend who once told me, "Don't complain. After all your stunts, you're not crippled and you still look good in your clothes." Well, I'm not crippled. This became a running joke in my life and oddly enough it got me through a few rough spots. Just being able to laugh at the absurdity of it all is comforting.

I want to make it clear that Warner Bros. and William Friedkin did not do me harm or misrepresent the truth. They simply repeated the publicity that was already out there, and it was widely accepted as truth at the time. I do not mean for anything I have said to insinuate that Warner Bros. or William Friedkin had anything to do with fabrication or misrepresentation. There is no way they could have known what was going on. It was a comedy of errors behind the scenes, and nobody was aware of it for years and years. I do not hold them responsible for any of this misunderstanding. It is not my intention to cast them in a negative light. That idea, if anyone has it, should be put to rest! Also, Warner Bros. did not give credit to anyone for the Spiderwalk. At that time, it was not traditional to give credit to stunt people.

Publicity and press do have a way of sometimes getting carried away. That's showbiz. All in all, people had fun with it and still do! So what the hell.

I take pride in the fact that I am standing up for myself against all odds. Living with truth in my life makes me happy. I will continue to tell the truth and stand up for myself. I am proud that my small contribution in William Friedkin's *The Exorcist (The Version You've Never Seen)* as well as the BBC documentary version made a big splash. Looking back makes me more grateful than ever for a dangerously exciting life for this girl from a small town in Arkansas!

About the Author

Ann "Annie" Miles grew up in Malvern, Arkansas, and started working professionally as a stunt performer at the Steel Pier in Atlantic City, New Jersey, at the age of seventeen. She attended Florida State University, training site for many Olympic gymnasts, on a gymnastics scholarship. During the 1960s and '70s, she was the busiest stuntwoman working on the East Coast and a top commercial model. She later became a hair stylist for TV, movies, and Broadway shows. Now retired from the entertainment business, Ann Miles spends most of her time writing.

Find her at IMDB: http://www.imdb.com/name/nm0587050 and on Facebook: @Ann.Annie.MilesStuntwoman.

CPSIA information can be obtained
at www.ICGtesting.com
Printed in the USA
FFOW04n1102220118

9 781945 624100